Chiswick House and Gardens

GREATER LONDON

RICHARD HEWLINGS

Chiswick House is a pioneer work in neoclassical architecture. It was designed by the Third Earl of Burlington (1694–1753), who sought to create the kind of house and garden that might have been found in the suburbs of ancient Rome. In this, Lord Burlington, the foremost architect of his generation, drew inspiration from similar attempts by the architects of sixteenth-century Italy. The text throws new light on the architectural design of Lord Burlington's enchanting villa and the interpretation of classical themes within the lay-out of the house and gardens.

English Heritage

LONDON

CONTENTS

The grounds of Chiswick House are owned by the London Borough of Hounslow.

Photographs of the House, unless otherwise credited, by the English Heritage Photographic Unit

Architectural terms used in the text are explained in the glossary (see page 61).

First published 1989
Printed in England by BAS Printers Limited, Over Wallop, Hampshire. C100. 2/89.

ISBN 1 85074 226 X

DESCRIPTION OF THE HOUSE

Introduction

The present house was built, probably in 1727–29, as an adjunct to an older one which stood immediately to its south-east. They were joined, probably in 1732–33, by a two-storey link building. The old house was demolished in 1788 and wings added either side of the present house. These were demolished in 1956–57.

Lord Burlington's house has two storeys. The ground floor is low, and simply ornamented, revealing its domestic and functional purpose. The first floor is high and richly ornamented, revealing its ceremonial and festive purpose. The plan of the house is a square, with an octagon inscribed in the centre. On the ground floor this octagon is a room called the Lower Tribune, the entrance hall. On the first floor it forms the Tribunal or Saloon, the principal reception room, which is carried up above the surrounding roof level and ceiled with a shallow dome. For direct access to the Saloon on ceremonial occasions a portico is at first-floor level, on the entrance side, approached by two flights of steps, each sub-divided to give the whole composition greater dignity.

The contents of the house are known from an inventory made in 1770, and they reveal what each room was intended for. So does the ornament, which, to the classically educated visitor, had easily understood meanings. These meanings, and the buildings from which Lord Burlington learned each ornamental feature, present, room by room, some idea of his architectural intentions.

Exterior

The columns of the portico are copied from an ancient Roman temple, the Temple of Castor and Pollux in Naples, of which Lord Burlington knew the illustration by the sixteenth-century Italian architect, Andrea Palladio. Lord Burlington's particular aim was to emulate the architecture of the ancient world, and he used sixteenth-century Italian architecture as an aid, on the assumption that it had realised the same aim more effectively than architecture before or since. The order of the portico is Corinthian, which theorists both ancient and sixteenth-century identified as maidenly. Sometimes it was associated with specifically female deities, such as Flora or Proserpine; more often unspecifically with the maidenly qualities of delicacy or refinement.

The shallow stepped dome is modelled on the ancient Roman Pantheon in Rome, but Lord Burlington was probably familiar also with its sixteenth-century Italian derivatives by Peruzzi, Palladio, Vignola and Scamozzi. The semi-circular windows below it, which light the central Saloon, are copied from windows in ancient Roman baths, particularly those called the Baths of Diocletian, and for this reason they are known as thermal or Diocletian windows. Lord Burlington would also have seen them used by the sixteenth-century Italians Raphael, Vignola, Palladio and Alessi.

The steps leading up to the portico have no apparent ancient prototype; in this case he may have invented their form by adversely criticising a similar portico designed by Palladio, whom he usually admired. They are ornamented by tooling the stone to make it resemble the volcanic stone (called tufa) in the neighbourhood of

Rome. He might have been less confident of employing this device for creating a resemblance to the buildings of the ancients had it not also been used by the sixteenth-century Italian architect Giulio Romano. Above the portico runs a band of wave-like ornament, called Vitruvian scroll. It is ornament of ancient origin, publicised in the sixteenth century by the Italian Sebastiano Serlio.

Short lengths of wall run east and west from the house surmounted by rows of ball-shaped finials. Whether such finials were used by the ancients is not known, but in the sixteenth century Michelangelo used ball finials to convey at least an ancient sensation, and in England ball finials of exactly this type were used by the early seventeenth-century architect Inigo Jones, who was equally anxious to recreate the arts of the ancient world. Jones's statue, and that of his mentor Andrea Palladio, stand in front of these walls: they were carved by Michael Rysbrack, and were first placed in a since-demolished garden building, before the present house was complete.

Around the corner, on the side elevations, the principal ornament is the central window. Its tripartite form is also not of ancient origin. But Lord Burlington would have known that it was invented by architects who were as fascinated by the ancients as he was. Its inventor was either Raphael or Giulio Romano, and it was used by their Italian followers, Vignola, Nanni di Baccio Bigio and Ammanati in Rome, Alessi in Genoa, Pellegrini in Milan, Sansovino in Venice, Palladio in Vicenza, and by the Italophile Jones in England. It was popularised in a text book by Serlio, and is therefore known as a *serliana*, but in England it is perversely also called a Venetian window. On the north elevation Lord Burlington used it three times, in a rarer form with a concentric relieving arch. This form was apparently invented by the sixteenth-century Italian Bramante, but Lord Burlington could also have known it in versions designed by Giulio, Palladio or Scamozzi.

In England the tapering form of the chimneys at Chiswick is unique. Only Lord Burlington's assistant Henry Flitcroft used them again, at Montagu House, Whitehall, now demolished. They are plainly derived from obelisks. Although of Egyptian origin, obelisks were indissolubly associated with ancient Rome, where a number had been set up as monumental ornaments. They were appreciated again in the sixteenth century, and in 1588–89 Pope Sixtus V re-erected those which had collapsed. These were all sited in prominent locations wihin the modern city, with inscriptions recording both their antiquity and the date of their re-erection, both of which would have inevitably recommended them to Lord Burlington. The obelisk form used as a chimney is much rarer, but Lord Burlington possessed a seventeenth-century drawing of the Palazzo Trissino in Vicenza, with obelisks prominently added as ornaments along the eaves line. Doubtless he adapted these ornaments as chimneys.

Ground Floor

The entrance below the portico and its stair is the one in use today, and is the one which would have been used for all but ceremonial or festive occasions. From the entrance a short passage leads to an internal room ringed with columns of the Tuscan order, known as the Lower Tribune. Two other passages approach this room from the east and west. Four peculiarities of this arrangement are based on recommendations or ideas of Palladio's. First, Palladio's book of architectural theory advised that the Tuscan order should only be used on the lowest floor.

The entrance to Chiswick House

Secondly, he particularly recommended it for 'atrios', which we might call vestibules. Thirdly, the internal octagon, lit only from the passages which approach it, is an arrangement unique to Palladio's Villa Almerico (the Rotonda) at Vicenza. Fourthly, the location of the four stairs hidden behind the diagonal walls of the central octagon was also suggested by the Villa Almerico. It may therefore be that the whole conception of the ground floor was suggested by Palladio's ideas. These include recommendations on the use of the rooms, on which Palladio wrote:

'All the well-contrived houses have in the middle . . . some places by which all

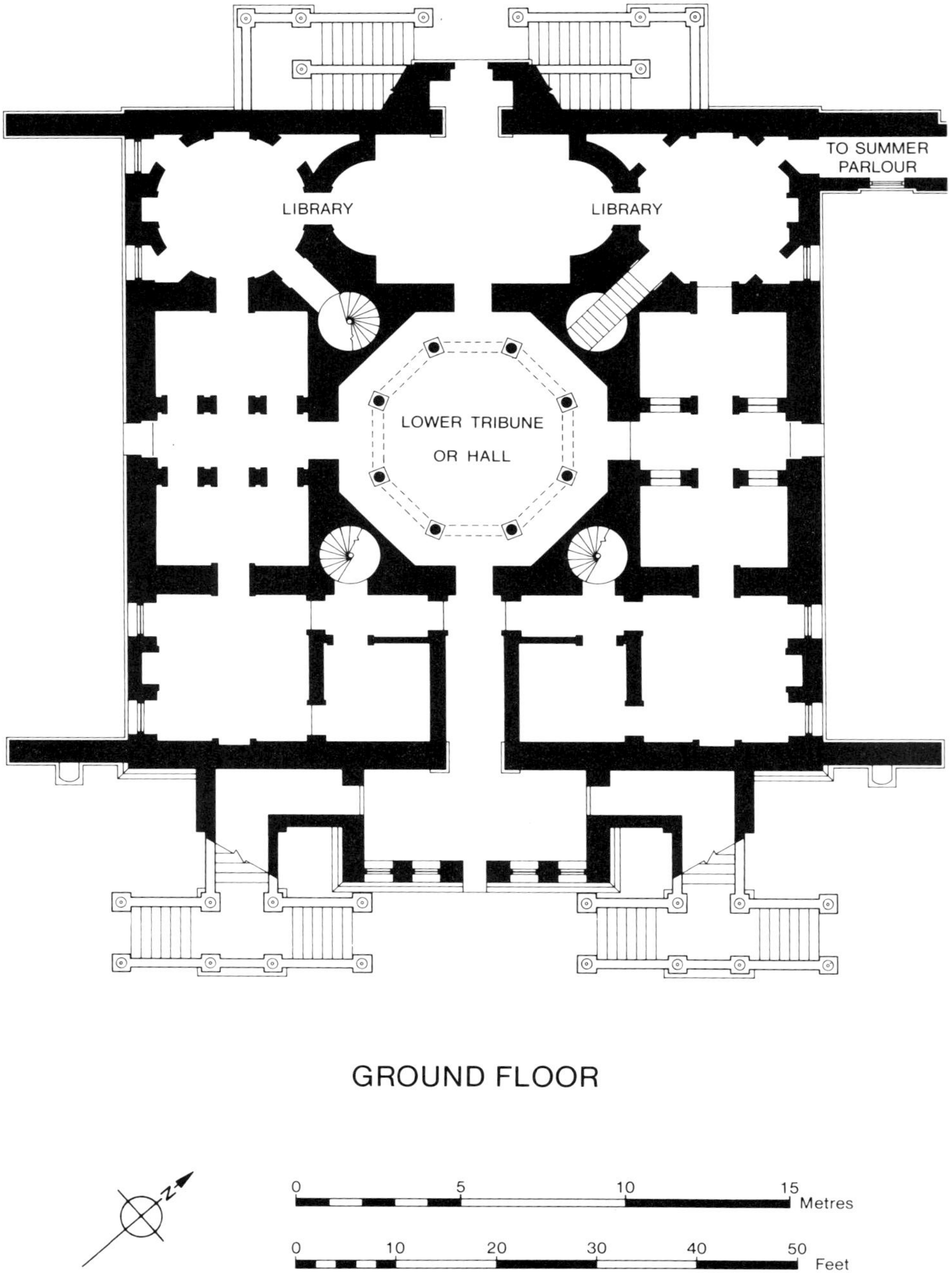

TO SUMMER PARLOUR

LIBRARY

LIBRARY

LOWER TRIBUNE OR HALL

GROUND FLOOR

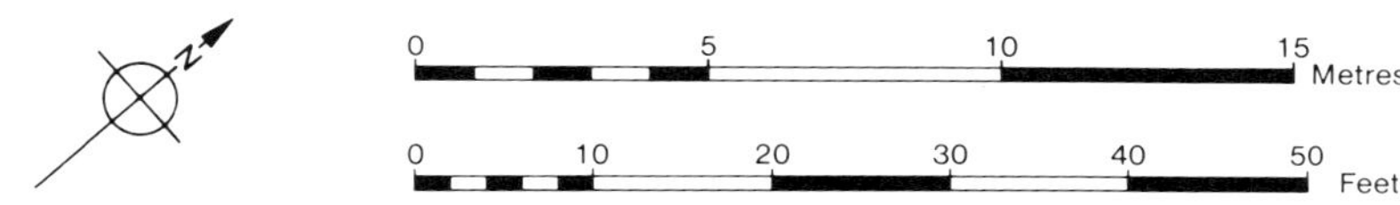

Plan of ground floor

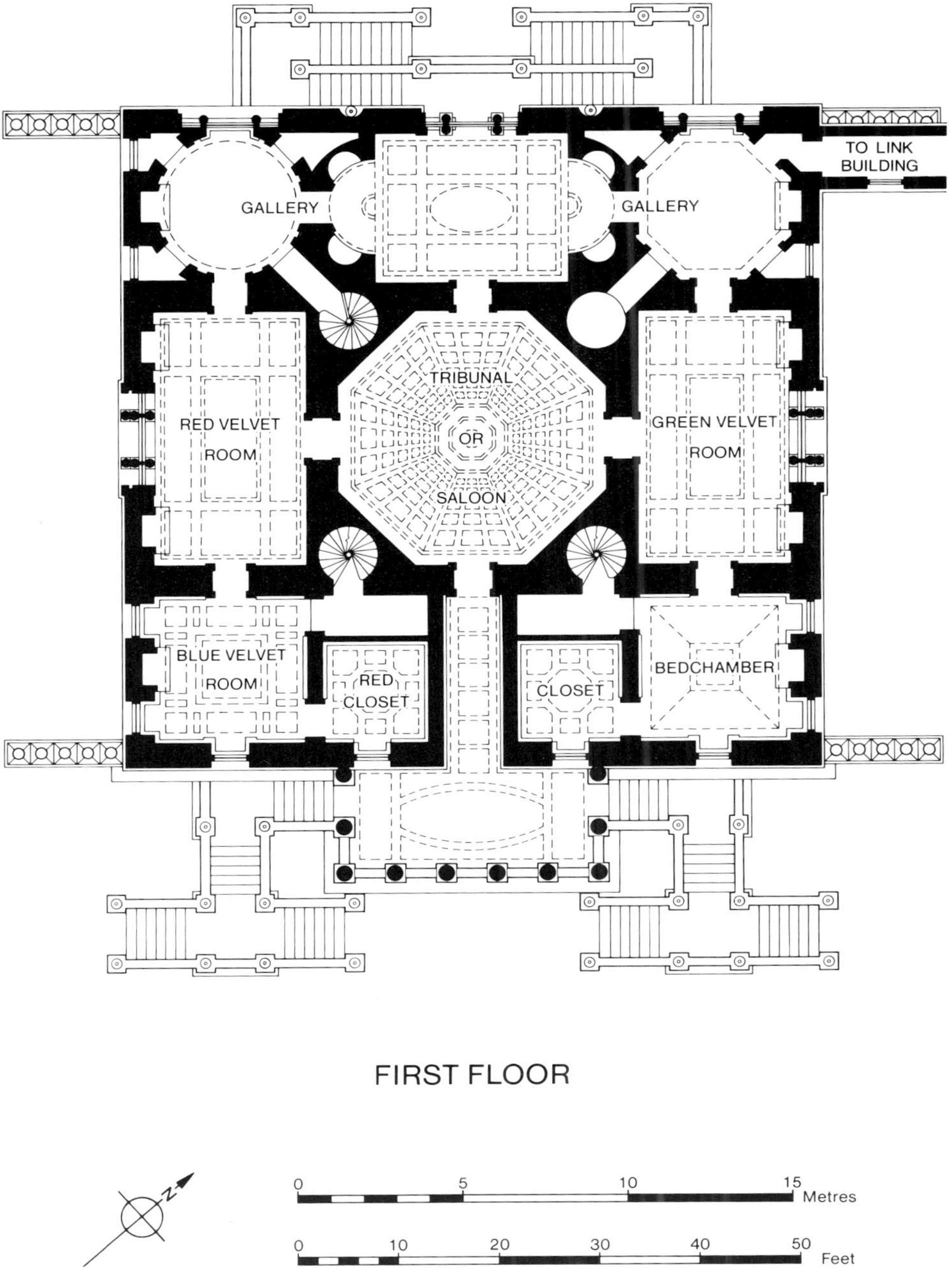

TO LINK BUILDING

GALLERY

GALLERY

TRIBUNAL OR SALOON

RED VELVET ROOM

GREEN VELVET ROOM

BLUE VELVET ROOM

RED CLOSET

CLOSET

BEDCHAMBER

FIRST FLOOR

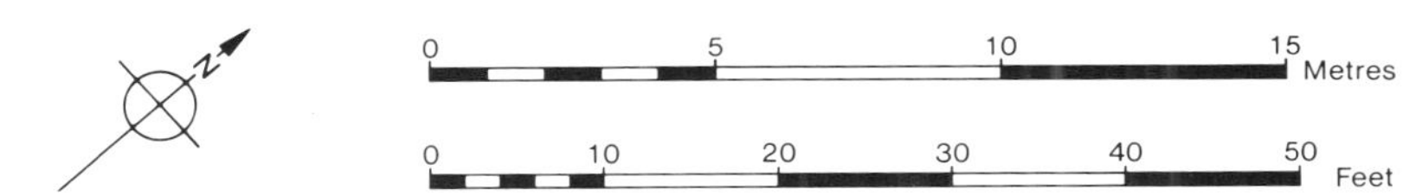

Plan of principal floor

> the others have a communication; these in the under part are called entries, and in the upper halls. These places are publick. The entries are the first parts, except the loggia's, which offer to those that enter the house, and are the most convenient to those who stay in who wait the master's coming out, to salute or do business with him'.

If Lord Burlington followed this advice, the Lower Tribune was intended as a waiting room, with Lord Burlington's business rooms or private apartment somewhere immediately adjacent. They cannot have been the rooms on the east side (not shown to the public), as these are plainly ornamented. But the rooms on the north and west sides, overlooking the garden, have dentilled cornices and carved enrichments to the door panels, all gilded.

The 1770 inventory confirms this speculation. The passage had two marble sideboards and eight walnut back stools. The Lower Tribune had twenty chairs and little else. Another room was a Butler's Pantry, containing £2,436 worth of plate. Another was called the Linen Room. These two were presumably those on the east side. The three northern rooms comprised the Library, with glass-fronted bookcases and reading tables. The remaining rooms, by elimination on the west side, were called the Bed Chambers and contained three four-post beds. It may have been from this apartment that Lord Burlington would have emerged to receive those waiting in the Lower Tribune.

Principal Floor

Access to the first floor is gained by a spiral stair leading off the west end of the Library, and this was the everyday access in Lord Burlington's time. But, since the first floor was the principal floor, lavishly ornamented, and containing two apartments of state, there was also a ceremonial access by the external stairs on the entrance front. From there a passage, open at the portico end, leads to a front door opening directly into the octagonal room at the centre of the building. Beyond this central room the northern part of the house is divided into three shaped rooms, all interconnecting: the western one is circular, the central one is rectangular with semi-circular apses at each end, and the eastern one is octagonal.

This plan is curious, unprecedented and not very clearly functional. Its intention can only have been to imitate the houses of the ancients. Sir John Clerk of Penicuik, visiting in 1729, described the house as 'all in the ancient manner'. The first feature he identified in evidence of this observation was the entrance passage. It is possible that Lord Burlington was aiming to recreate a feature of the ancient Greek house, described by the Roman author Vitruvius as having 'passageways for people entering from the front, not very wide, . . . shut off by doors at the inner end'. The three interconnecting rooms on the north side, however, are intended to recall the geometrically-shaped rooms of the baths of ancient Rome.

Modern visitors take the everyday route by the newel stair to the principal floor. Using the plan, they are advised to make their way first to the central room.

Tribunal or Saloon

This room was called 'a large Tribunal' by Sir John Clerk in 1727, and the 'Saloon' in the 1770 inventory. Palladio, in his words quoted on page 5, would have styled it a hall. He described the function of a hall as:

> '. . . for feasts entertainment and decorations, for comedies, weddings and such like recreations'.

The 1770 inventory suggests that the use recommended by Palladio was followed by Lord Burlington. It was sparsely, but grandly furnished with four

Bust of emperor in the Tribunal

giltwood tables with marble tops, each flanked by a pair of hall chairs. A description in 1761 lists antique busts on brackets, and the same paintings which are there today, except for *Lord Burlington and his three sisters* by Kneller, which is now at Chatsworth. Its place is taken by Guido Reni's *Liberality and Modesty*, which formerly hung in the dining-room of the old house.

In consequence of this evidently festive and ceremonial use, the order in this room is Composite, the most festive and the highest in status. The room is ceiled by a dome divided into octagonal plaster coffers. This ornament was intended to look antique, for an annotated sketch by Lord Burlington's clerk reveals that the pattern was copied from the ancient Roman Basilica of Maxentius. Originally it was 'interspersed with gilding'. The room is lit from the drum of the dome by windows derived from the ancient Roman Baths of Diocletian.

Evidently, therefore, his intention was to recreate an ancient interior. But he was doubtless encouraged in doing so by the examples of the sixteenth-century Italians, Palladio, whose plan he adapted, and Alessi, who used similar octagonal coffering.

Gallery

The three rooms north of the Saloon have been known as the Gallery since 1761. But this must not be understood as a picture gallery, since the 1770 inventory lists only six paintings there, and an 1820 watercolour reveals that they were 'skyed': three being above the windows where the light would have prevented them from being seen. Nor can it have been intended as a viewing gallery over the garden, for the present view, down to the *exedra*, only came into existence between 1733 and 1736. Until then the trees of the Grove grew to within ten feet of the windows.

We can therefore turn only to the evidence of the rooms themselves to explain their use. No doors close the arches between the central room and those to east and west. That all three were conceived as one is confirmed by the inventory, which makes no distinction between them. Their intercommunicating plan—a circle, rectangle with apses, and octagon – is taken from the Baths of Diocletian, and is therefore intended to look antique. The lozenge-shaped coffering in the apses is copied from the Temple of Venus and Roma. But the combination of room shapes had already been revived in sixteenth-century Italy: Bramante and Peruzzi used it in their proposals for rebuilding the Basilica of St Peter in Rome, which were well-known through their publication by Serlio. The shape of the central room in particular had been used by Raphael, Giulio, Peruzzi, Sangallo, Vignola and Palladio, and in such circumstances would

The Gallery, looking towards the Octagonal Room

be more suggestive of sixteenth-century Italy than of ancient Rome. The Italian architects had used this room-shape for loggias, rooms which were usually open on one side to a garden or small court, and often ornamented with sculpture rather than painting. Among them, Raphael, Giulio, Sangallo and Palladio had built loggias in exactly this position in the house, diametrically opposite the entrance. One of Palladio's loggias had been glazed, as this is; in Palladio's case, because it was in a town house without a garden; in this case, as a concession to the English climate. It is

Ceiling of the Gallery central room, depicting the Relief of Smyrna

difficult, therefore, to resist the conclusion that a room of this shape, located at a point where the garden almost invaded the house, and ornamented by substantial pieces of sculpture, was intended as a loggia, a room whose use was described by Palladio 'as to walk, eat in, and other recreations'. And a plan of the house made in 1788 shows that the south-western and south-eastern cupboards, opening off the Round and Octagonal Rooms respectively, were water closets.

The central room of the three has a flat ceiling with an oval painting of the Relief of Smyrna. The painted ornament around it (which may be by William Kent) illustrates various martial themes. Lord Burlington held the post of Captain of the Band of Gentlemen Pensioners from 1731 to 1733. The Gentlemen Pensioners (now the Honourable Company of Gentlemen at Arms) were the second oldest military formation in the kingdom, with the responsibility of attending the King personally in battle, and mounting guard in the Presence Chamber at all times. If the military theme of this ceiling alludes to any aspect of Lord Burlington's life this short tenure of military office must be it. However, in 1761 the *Relief of Smyrna* was described as by Veronese. If that was Lord Burlington's belief, it may have been bought as the work of a great master, irrespective of its subject matter. The subjects of the surrounding ornament would in that case have been painted to complement the painting rather than the patron.

The Octagonal Room, looking through to the Green Velvet Room

Certainly the remaining ornament does not fit a military theme. The four statues in the niches represent Venus, Mercury, Apollo and a Muse. The present ones are casts, but, of the originals, the first two were by G B Guelfi (whom Lord Burlington encouraged to come from Italy), the second two by Peter Scheemakers. The two huge porphyry vases were bought in Rome on 4 February 1715.

The order in the Gallery, as in nearly all the principal floor rooms, is Corinthian. In the Round and Octagonal Rooms the walls are ornamented with festoons of flowers issuing from woven baskets supported on female heads. The distinctive feature of these baskets is the leaves sprouting from their sides. That must represent the story recounted by Vitruvius of the origin of the Corinthian capital, whereby a basket inadvertently placed on top of an acanthus plant eventually breaks into leaf. Vitruvius described the Corinthian as an order possessed of feminine qualities; so here are young women who support the baskets. Evidently these two rooms were intended to contain an allegory of the Corinthian order.

Red Velvet Room

The rooms on the west and east sides of the house form identical sets of apartments, entered from the Round and Octagonal Rooms of the Gallery, respectively. The west apartment, overlooking the garden, is more richly ornamented and has painted ceilings. Both were evidently apartments of state, the west one of higher status. What

Ceiling of the Red Velvet Room, representing a triumph of the arts

both have in common is that the principal room of each was used as a picture gallery, for both red and green velvet were regarded as the most suitable background for pictures.

The principal room of the west apartment is the Red Velvet Room. Unlike the Gallery, which only had six paintings, the Red Velvet Room held twenty-eight. They were almost all of religious or mythological subjects, and were clearly the major paintings of Lord Burlington's collection. As was appropriate for such a use, the furniture was sparse. The room only contained 'two fine marble tables with brass mouldings on gilt frames' and '8 gilt back stools, cover'd with velvet and serge cases'.

The ceiling is painted with an allegory appropriate to a room hung with valuable paintings. It is divided into nine panels. The central panels at each end contain portrait busts flanked by a flute and a trumpet (at the north), and a harp and lute (at the south). All four instruments could represent music. Alternatively they could represent music (north) and poetry (south), or different modes of poetry (Tragic, Comic, Epic and Lyric). The panels along the sides illustrate six of the seven presiding deities with their zodiacal houses (and in four cases their alternative houses). On the west side, from south to north, are Jupiter, Venus and Saturn. On the east side are Mars, Diana and Apollo.

The seventh deity, Mercury, fills the centre panel. Mercury, as a messenger, represents commerce, and behind him therefore stands Abundance emptying her cornucopia. He also represents the Arts, and his children are usually painters, orators and players.

Painting and the theatre were the Burlingtons' particular interests. Here Mercury directs the cornucopia to the three visual arts. Painting is represented by a portrait of Kent, Sculpture by a bust of Inigo Jones, fallen and awaiting resurrection, and Architecture by the ground plan of a Roman temple, that of Fortuna Virilis (male fortune). The composition is evidently intended as an allegory of all the arts, with the visual ones in pride of place. The painter was almost certainly William Kent.

Blue Velvet Room

To the south is the next room in the apartment, called the Blue Velvet Room. In the standard state apartment of the day the middle room would be the bedchamber. So it was in the eastern apartment at Chiswick: but not here. The 1770 inventory lists eight particularly splendid tapestry chairs around the walls, an inlaid black marble side-board table, and, instead of a bed, a library table with rounded ends. The room held twenty-six paintings, almost as many as the much larger preceding room. Inevitably they must have been smaller paintings, and they were in fact landscapes, mainly Dutch. It sounds as if the room was a cabinet, intended for the entertainment of connoisseurs.

What kind of connoisseurs they may have been is made clear by the allegorical figures painted on the ceiling by William Kent. The central figure represents Architecture. She has a Corinthian capital as a crown. She is surrounded by boys carrying drawing instruments. Plumb lines are painted on the vertical members. Four more Corinthian capitals are painted on the soffits of the beams. Lord Burlington used one of the garden buildings as a drawing office, so these architectural representations did not preside over the creating of architectural designs. Instead they may have presided over their display. For Isaac Ware claimed that he was shown Lord Burlington's famous collection of architectural drawings in his lordship's 'Study'.

It is difficult to find a room in an ancient house which corresponds to a connoisseur's study. So Lord Burlington was obliged to turn to an Italian Renaissance prince's house for an architectural model. The most striking features of the room are the unusually large *cyma reversa* brackets supporting the ceiling. They are copied from either (or both) of two sixteenth-century prototypes, a *studiolo* in the palace of the Duke of Mantua, and the other a drawing by Cherubino Alberti.

Ceiling of the Blue Velvet Room, representing an allegory of architecture

Red Closet

The final room of the west apartment lies east of the Blue Velvet Room. It is called the Red Closet from its former crimson lutestring (glazed silk) hangings. Although the smallest room of the three, it held the most paintings, thirty-six, presumably the smallest and most precious. It held another library table, a small mahogany table, and four gilt armchairs covered with crimson silk damask. Four chairs to the Blue Velvet Room's eight indicates that this room was still more intimate, and its numerous small possessions presumably still more precious.

Green Velvet Room

The east apartment can be reached by returning to the Red Velvet Room and crossing the Saloon. The principal room, corresponding to the Red Velvet Room, is called the Green Velvet Room. Like the former, it appears to have been intended to hang the best paintings. Green and red velvet were both regarded as suitable backgrounds. The Green Velvet Room held twenty-five paintings in 1761 (compared with twenty-eight in the Red Velvet Room), and their subjects were mainly mythological. But it also held some landscapes and domestic scenes, usually considered a lower order of subject matter. The furniture was also comparable: to the Red Velvet Room's two marble-topped tables, the Green Velvet Room had two *Boulle* tables.

Bedchamber

The room south of the Green Velvet Room was the state bedchamber. In it Lady Burlington died in 1758. The walls were hung with Brussels tapestries, illustrating a Village Fête scene by Teniers. The bed was hung with needlework, lined and fringed with crimson lutestring. There were also two gilt settees covered with crimson silk damask, two Siena marble slabs on gilt stands and a French commode with brass gilt ornaments. The hearth had silver dogs and hearth furniture. It was the only room to have tapestry hangings and silver hearth furniture, and it was evidently the most sumptuously appointed room in the house.

Bedchamber Closet

West of the Bedchamber is the last room in the east apartment. Like the Red Closet in the west apartment, the Bedchamber Closet was hung with an abundance of pictures. It had twenty-two Italian views by Gaspare degli Occhiale, and, later, some fancy pictures from the Red Closet were added. The furniture consisted of a walnut bureau, a walnut bookcase, a mahogany tripod table, a pot cupboard and two gilt armchairs upholstered in silk damask. Evidently it was used for writing, presumably by Lady Burlington, and the presence of only two chairs indicates that it was even more intimate than the Red Closet (which had four).

Link Building

There is one other room on the first floor, and that is the building which was constructed in 1732–33 to link the house of 1727–29 with the old house which stood further east. It is reached from the Octagonal Room of the Gallery. Since 1957 it has been a dead end. The room was unheated, so it may only have had a processional function. It had three marble tables on gilt stands, one of which was round and therefore presumably free-standing, and eight elbow chairs covered with leather.

Although probably not a room which was lingered in, the high status suggested by the marble gilt tables is confirmed by the decoration. It is the only room apart from the Saloon to have a Composite order. It was possible for Lord Burlington to find an antique source for rooms of largely processional intent. Using the baths of ancient Rome as a model he sub-divided the room with two colonnades, which are open above their entablatures. The colonnades are Corinthian because they form a secondary order within a Composite scheme. Although the resemblance to ancient Roman architecture was undoubtedly his intention, it was not his only source for this feature. In sixteenth-century Italy such screens of columns had been used by Bramante, Peruzzi, Palladio, Vasari and Buontalenti.

The ceiling in this room is closely modelled on a drawing in Lord Burlington's possession of the ceiling of an ancient Roman building at Pozzuoli near Naples. The draughtsman, who is unknown, was a late sixteenth or early seventeenth-century Italian. This drawing is a clear instance of Lord Burlington's desire to create a house in the ancient style and of how he used sixteenth-century Italian architects as a source of information about the ancient world.

The room in the ground floor of the Link Building has since 1957 to be reached by returning down the newel stairs in the main part of the house. Like the room above, it is divided by screens of columns, but these are Tuscan to accord with the rest of the ground floor. From its east end the Summer Parlour can be reached via a corridor made in 1957.

Summer Parlour or Garden Room

In the plan made by John White in 1788 this room is called the Garden Room, and the plan shows a 'China Closet' opening off its east end. It must therefore be identifiable with 'The Garden Room and Closet' in the 1770 inventory, and with the room styled 'Lady Burlington's Dressing Room, built at her own Expence . . . the China-Closet within it' by Horace Walpole in 1760. Walpole described this room in greater detail than any of the others. In the 1770 inventory its contents are worth nearly twice that of any other in the house.

Why this should be so is not clear, but the room's high status is made manifest by its ceiling, the only one with decorative painting on the ground floor and on the east side of the house. The connection which Walpole makes with Lady Burlington is confirmed by the owl devices painted in the corners of the ceilings, for the owl was the heraldic badge of the Saviles, Lady Burlington's family. The ceiling is painted in a manner known as grotesque. It was not easy to discover how such rooms were decorated in the ancient world, but, for Lord Burlington, the method used in sixteenth-century Rome was good enough. The foremost example was the decorative scheme invented by Raphael in the Vatican Palace, consisting of small panels with naturalistic scenes, connected by fronds of stylised vegetation painted in a limited colour range. The painter William Kent, who had lived in Rome from 1709 to 1719, had mastered this style, and one of the first jobs he had on returning to England was to paint a grotesque ceiling at Kensington Palace, a commission which was engineered by Lord Burlington. It therefore seems likely that he was also responsible for the ceiling in the Summer Parlour at Chiswick.

He also designed the original chimney-piece in this room, illustrated in John Vardy's *Some Designs of Mr Inigo Jones and Mr William Kent* in 1744, with the caption '. . . at Cheswick . . . W. Kent Invt.'. This chimney-piece is now at Chatsworth and the chimney-piece in its place comes from one of the wings built in 1788. Indeed Kent may have been responsible for more, because a letter from Brian Fairfax to Lady Burlington says that 'The Prince . . . has sent for His architect [Kent] to begin His building. I wish Yr Ladyps Room meets with no delay from it.' The letter is dated 26 August 1735, a time when Lady Burlington was buying furniture for this room.

The room was furnished with twelve very expensive giltwood elbow chairs, supplied by the upholsterer Stephen Langley in April 1735. There was also a pair of mahogany commodes, with giltwood pier glasses, supplied by the cabinet maker John Boson in September 1735. They, too, bore Lady Burlington's owl device, and can be seen in a sketch of Lady Burlington drawing. There was also a tripod reading table, and Walpole's list of pictures consists entirely of portraits (mainly of relatives), some of which were miniatures, some sketches, and some in crayons. The evidence of drawing, reading and family pictures suggests a very private room, and it was, of course, a little isolated from both the old and the new houses.

DESCRIPTION OF THE GARDENS

Whether the modern visitor approaches by Duke's Avenue (in the north-east), Corney Road Lodge (in the south-east), or the Burlington Lane Gate (in the south-west), it is best to begin a tour of the gardens opposite the south front of the house. If the following route is then pursued, an approximate equivalence to the historic development can be maintained, falling into four broad phases:

1. Lord Burlington's garden up to 1727
2. Lord Burlington's additions after 1727
3. Fifth Duke of Devonshire's changes, 1764–1811
4. Sixth Duke of Devonshire's additions, 1811–58

Suggested routes for visitors through the gardens, beginning at the south front of the house. The tours roughly follow the chronological development of the gardens:

up to 1727
after 1727
after 1764
after 1811

Lord Burlington's garden up to 1727

The present avenue on the south side of the house is nearly three times the length of Lord Burlington's forecourt. Until 1818 the road passed much closer to the house, and the forecourt, whose south end was semi-circular, was closed by a pair of stone piers decorated with vermiculated rustication and a band of fretwork, and surmounted by sphinxes. This arrangement is shown existing by 1728 in Pieter Andreas Rysbrack's painting, and, in more detail, in Jacques Rigaude's drawing of 1733 (see page 38). The original piers, after several moves, ended up in Green Park, London. The present piers and forecourt design were moved to this location *c* 1950 from a position on the Sixth Duke of Devonshire's drive.

Lord Burlington's intention was to recreate the sort of garden which he

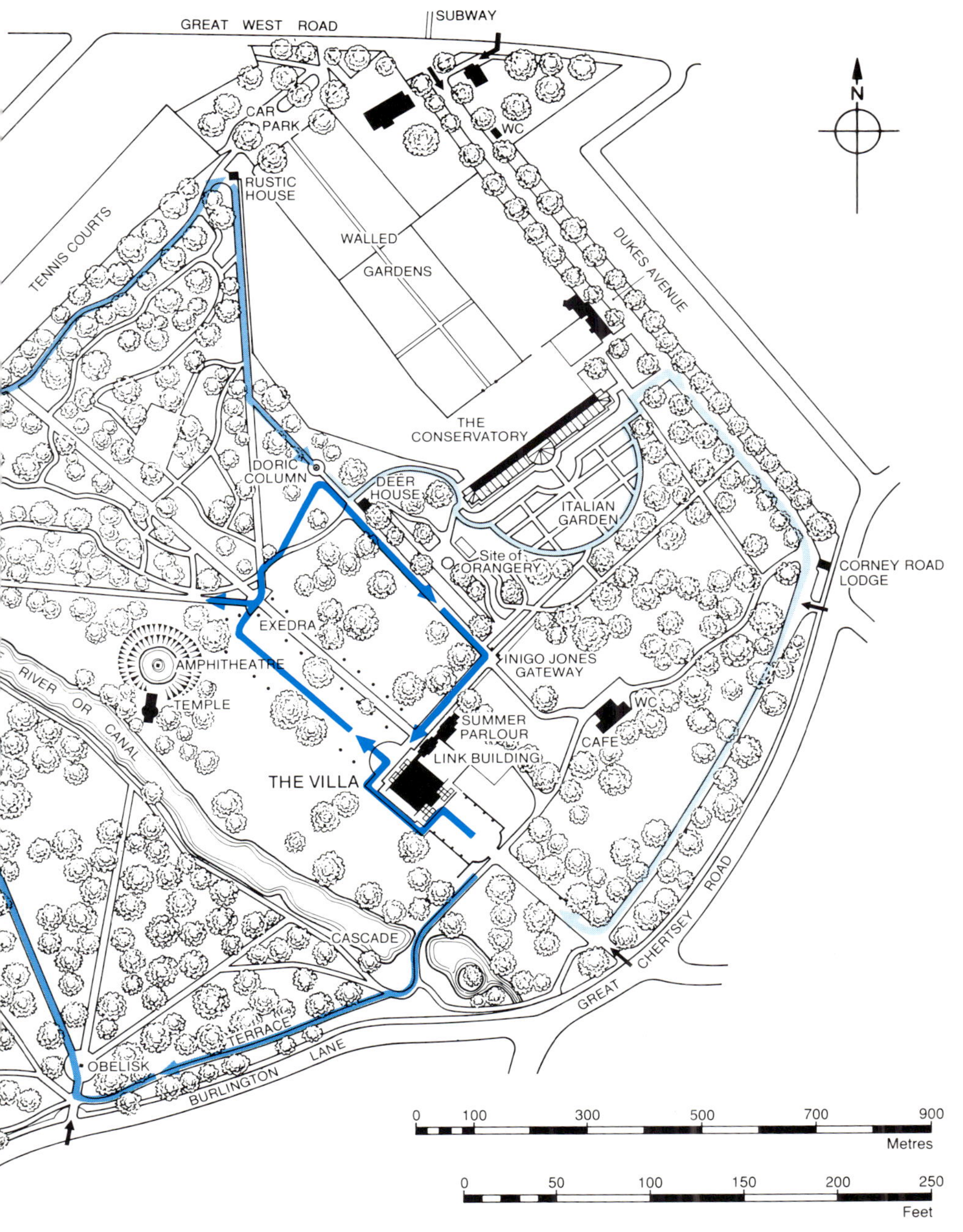
GREAT WEST ROAD
SUBWAY
N
CAR PARK
WC
RUSTIC HOUSE
TENNIS COURTS
WALLED GARDENS
DUKES AVENUE
THE CONSERVATORY
DORIC COLUMN
DEER HOUSE
ITALIAN GARDEN
Site of ORANGERY
CORNEY ROAD LODGE
EXEDRA
INIGO JONES GATEWAY
AMPHITHEATRE
RIVER OR CANAL
TEMPLE
WC
SUMMER PARLOUR
CAFE
LINK BUILDING
THE VILLA
CASCADE
GREAT CHERTSEY ROAD
TERRACE
OBELISK
BURLINGTON LANE
0 100 300 500 700 900
Metres
0 50 100 150 200 250
Feet

believed would have existed in the ancient world. He was evidently influenced by a book dedicated to him by its author, Robert Castell, in 1728, called *Villas of the Ancients*. One of the distinctive features of Castell's reconstructions of ancient gardens were enclosures with semi-circular terminations. The information on which such reconstructions were based was also influenced by Bramante, Raphael and Vignola, Roman architects of the sixteenth-century who had also designed gardens with semi-circular terminations in the belief that this was a feature of ancient villa gardens.

The piers themselves were ornamented by bands of fretwork ornament. The origin of this type of ornament is also ancient Roman, and that is doubtless why Lord Burlington used it. But he was probably encouraged to do so by its frequent employment in sixteenth-century Italy. It was used by Peruzzi, Giulio Romano, Antonio da Sangallo the younger, and Galeazzo Alessi, and it was illustrated by the architectural writers Serlio and Palladio.

The only parts of the forecourt piers which were not restored *c* 1950 were the finial sculptures, in the form of sphinxes. Two more sphinxes were placed north of the house, probably by 1742, and a third in 1748. Lord Burlington's forecourt sphinxes were unprecedented in England. But there were also sphinxes at Castle Hill, Devon, a house designed by him in 1729, and sphinxes at Leeswood hall, Clwyd, designed by an unknown architect in the 1730s. They were to become a favourite motif of Robert Adam later in the century. It is possible Lord Burlington associated them with ancient Rome, but there are not many ancient Roman examples.

However, he may well have associated them with sixteenth-century Rome. Roman artists and architects of that period whose work reflects an interest in Egyptology were numerous: they included Giuliano da Sangallo, Pinturicchio, Nanni da Viterbo, Mantegna, Bramante, Pirro Ligorio, Raphael and Giulio Romano. At least one Roman tomb of that period incorporates sphinxes, and so did Primaticcio's paintings at Fontainebleau.

They were not intended just as a novel form of ornament. Their meaning would have been clear to any of Lord Burlington's classically educated contemporaries. The sphinx in Greek mythology guarded Thebes and let no travellers pass who could not answer its riddle. Whenever it occurred in classical art it represented wisdom. Outside Chiswick House the sphinxes were perhaps intended to signify that the visitor entered a house of ancient and arcane mysteries.

The forecourt is lined by *termini*, stone piers ending in sculptured human faces. These were here by at least 1733 (when Rigaud drew them), but in 1814 the Sixth Duke of Devonshire moved them further south, to line his new avenue. They were returned here *c* 1950. This feature is also of Roman origin, but, again, was used frequently in sixteenth-century Italy, by Pirro Ligorio, Vignola, Alessi and Giacomo della Porta.

On the west side of the house a lawn falls down towards the so-called River. This lawn was a necessary consequence of the building of the house in 1727–29: the principal apartment was on the west side, demanding a view, and the north side was hemmed in by the trees of the Grove, initially coming to within ten feet of the house. The lawn was made in stages. The part immediately west of the house was complete by *c* 1728. South of it Lord Burlington planted a maze, but by 1742 he had grubbed this up, and extended the lawn south. The northernmost part of the west lawn once held a rectangular piece of water with semi-circular projections. This was in existence by *c* 1728, but was filled

Pieter Andreas Rysbrack. Chiswick House seen from the Terrace, c *1728*

George Lambert. Chiswick House seen from top of the Cascade in 1742

John Donowell. Chiswick House and the Cascade, from west side of the River, 1753

in by the Fifth Duke of Devonshire, who extended the lawn over it in 1772.

North of the house stood the Grove, a plantation of trees regularly and closely spaced. It was in existence by 1727, when its closeness to the house was commented on. From then on it was progressively eliminated. By *c* 1728 a semi-circular clearing had been made in front of the house, and demarcated by an iron railing. Between 1733 and 1736 a swath, of the same width as the house, was cut northwards through the Grove, terminating in a semi-circular recess,

Pieter Andreas Rysbrack. One of the two ponds and the Grove, from north-west, c *1728*

Jacques Rigaud. The Grove and Chiswick House, seen from future exedra site in 1733

called the *exedra*. By 1742 all the western half of the Grove had been felled, and the *exedra* was linked to the house by two lines of stone urns, with a third line of stone urns on the far (eastern) side of the path which had once divided the Grove from north to south. The eastern half of the Grove remained, progressively diminishing throughout the nineteenth century.

The path which, as mentioned above, sub-divided the Grove, actually pre-dated it and everything else now remaining. It was in existence in 1707. The Sixth Duke of Devonshire turfed it over, and in the 1880s the Marquess of Bute made a new

Jacques Rigaud. The Grove, the southern Deer House, the Summer Parlour, the Link Building and Chiswick House, seen from the north-west in 1733

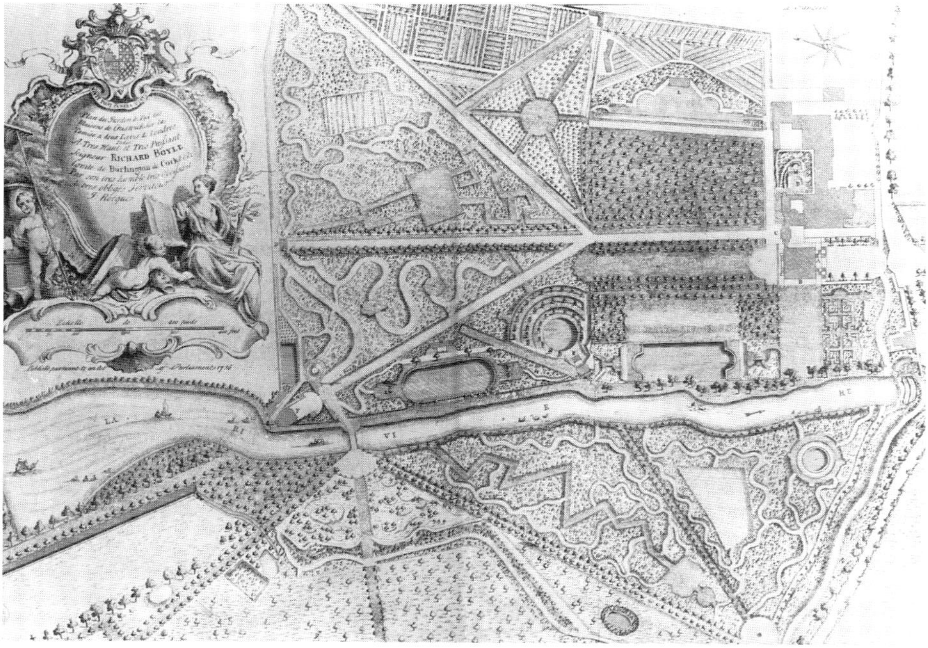

John Rocque. Plan of the garden at Chiswick in 1736

George Lambert. The eastern half of the Grove, the Inigo Jones Gate, the Summer Parlour, the Link Building and Chiswick House, seen from the north-west in 1742

John Donowell. The exedra, seen from the north perron of Chiswick House in 1753

path, a little to the west, aligned on the centre of the north front, and terminating in an oval in the centre of the *exedra*. This was removed and the original path was restored *c* 1950.

The *exedra* is another semi-circular termination, presumably intended, like that in the forecourt, to resemble the gardens of the ancient Romans, as illustrated in Castell's *Villas of the Ancients*. But again Lord Burlington must have been encouraged to venture this particular piece of archaeological reconstruction by earlier attempts in sixteenth-century Italy, such as those at Villa Aldobrandini, Frascati, or the Villas Mattei and Pamphili in Rome.

The statuary in the *exedra* is a mixture of ancient and modern. The flanking statues are of lions, next in are *termini* (three of which represent Socrates, Lycurgus and Lucius Verus), next come two urns. The lions were described by Defoe in 1742, and the whole group was in position by 1753 at the latest. The three central figures were brought to their present location from elsewhere, however. In 1728 an anonymous French traveller recorded seeing them in the Ionic Temple. But they were moved to the *exedra* by 1738, when Defoe identified them as having been unearthed at Hadrian's Villa in Tivoli. That was confirmed by Dodsley, writing in 1761, and by Faulkner in 1845, who adds a probably fanciful identification of them as Cicero, Pompey and Caesar. The identification of the *termini*, however, is certain, since their names are inscribed. Socrates, Lycurgus and Lucius Verus have, in common, their practical opposition to tyranny. Between the Excise Crisis of 1732 and the resignation of Sir Robert Walpole in 1742, tyranny and Walpole's alleged moves towards it were topical subjects, especially among those members of the nobility who felt that they were excluded from what they believed to be their rightful place in government. Lord Cobham, who had resigned from government at the same moment as Lord

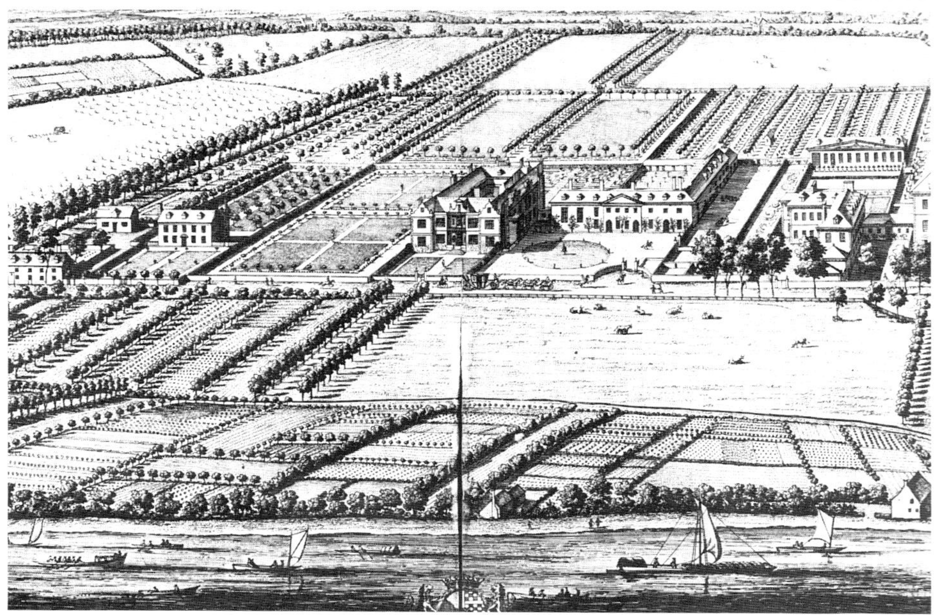

Leonard Knyff. The gardens and old house at Chiswick, from the south-east in 1707

Burlington, constructed an entire garden at Stowe, his estate in Buckinghamshire, on the themes of Liberty and Tyranny. The *exedra* at Chiswick was presumably conceived with the same purpose.

To the east of the *exedra*, the central path across the former Grove terminates in a *patte d'oie* (French for goose's foot) whence three avenues radiated. The *patte d'oie* and its avenues were certainly completed by 1728 (when they were recorded in two paintings by P A Rysbrack), probably by 1719, and were possibly under construction in 1717 (when the building which terminated the west avenue was built). All three avenues terminated in buildings, the *Casina* at the end of the westerly one, the Pagan Temple at the end of the central one, and the Rustic House at the end of the easterly one. The *Casina* was pulled down by the Fifth Duke of Devonshire in 1778, and the Pagan Temple by 1784. On the advice of his gardener, Samuel Lapidge (Capability Brown's former assistant and professional heir), the Duke replaced the westerly and central avenues with serpentine walks. The avenues were restored *c* 1950.

The Rustic House is some way distant, and therefore perhaps best seen later in the tour, between the Fifth Duke's wilderness, and the Sixth Duke's Italian garden. It is an arched alcove, ornamented with rusticated stone. This form of ornament was thought appropriate for grottoes, buildings intended to simulate the dwellings of wood or water nymphs. In a conventionally Christian society which did not believe in such creatures, grottoes can only have been intended as poetic or even whimsical allusions to the gardens of pagan Rome. But, although the Latin authors may have described grottoes, their detailed form could only be guessed at. Inevitably Lord Burlington was guided by previous generations who had attempted to

Pieter Andreas Rysbrack. Statue of Samson slaying the Philistine, the Casina and the Pagan Temple, seen from the patte d'oie, c *1728*

Pieter Andreas Rysbrack. The Rustic House, the Doric Column and the northern Deer House, seen from the patte d'oie, c *1728*

John Donowell. The Casina, Pagan Temple and Rustic House, seen from the patte d'oie in 1753

reconstruct ancient grottoes. There were numerous sixteenth-century grottoes around Rome and Genoa. Under the influence of the Italophile architect Inigo Jones, a few had also been constructed in early seventeenth-century England, notably at Greenwich, Woburn and Wilton. Lord Burlington's Rustic House was not intended to be quite the same as these, but he chose rusticated masonry as a suitable form of ornament. For its detailing he probably used the rustication illustrated by the sixteenth-century Italian architectural writer Sebastiano Serlio.

West of the *patte d'oie* and west of the *exedra*, only reached from the westerly radiating avenue, is the Orange Tree Garden. It was shown in its completed form by P A Rysbrack in 1728, and the Ionic Temple which forms part of it was illustrated in William Kent's *Designs of Inigo Jones* in 1727. It takes the form of an amphitheatre surrounding a circular pool, in which stands an obelisk. Orange trees were placed in tubs on the steps of the amphitheatre. Behind the pool stands the Ionic Temple. The amphitheatre is, by definition, intended to simulate the architecture of ancient Rome. So is the obelisk, for although obelisks are of Egyptian origin, a few were transported from Egypt and re-erected in Rome during Imperial times. The Ionic Temple is distinctive for having a circular body with a rectangular temple portico attached. It is apparently based on one of two ancient Roman examples, the Pantheon or the Temple of Romulus. But there were also sixteenth-century Italian variants of this form of temple, designed by Pirro Ligorio, Serlio and Palladio. In 1728 the Ionic Temple housed the three antique statues now in the *exedra*.

From the *patte d'oie*, a subsidiary avenue immediately south of the main easterly one leads to the Doric Column. This might be the 'pillar or obelisk' mentioned by Sir John Clerk of Penicuik, a Scottish visitor, in 1727, but it was certainly built by 1728 when P A Rysbrack recorded it in a painting. An undated sketch in the hand of William Kent shows

Pieter Andreas Rysbrack. The Orange Tree Garden, Obelisk Pond and the Temple, seen from the north, c *1728. A photograph of the present-day garden appears on page 57*

a copy of the Venus de Medici on its top. The intention, both of the column and the copy of a well-known classical statue, was evidently to produce an ancient Roman effect. Lord Burlington might have been inspired by similar free-standing classical columns in Italian gardens. The Sixth Duke of Devonshire's gardener, Lewis Kennedy, laid out a rose garden around it in concentric rings, which was still there when recorded for the Marquess of Bute in the 1880s.

A path leads south from the Doric Column to the Deer House, which was the northerly of a pair. The Deer House is shown on a painting by Rysbrack of 1728, and its southern counterpart on a drawing by Rigaud of 1733. From here a ha-ha (sunk fence) borders the east side of a path running south to the Inigo Jones gateway, on the site of a second deer house. The deer lived in a paddock to the east. When Lord Burlington acquired the property called Sutton Court, west of the so-called River, in 1727, he made a deer park there, freeing this paddock for other uses. He converted it to an orange tree garden, with hedges either side stepping back to an orangery. Rocque's view dated 1733 and Rigaud's dated 1736 show alternative designs for this building, but the design

Plan of the garden at Chiswick House during the tenure of the Marquess of Bute, between 1881 and 1892

John Donowell. The northern Deer House, the Orangery, the Inigo Jones Gate (all seen through the eastern half of the Grove), and the rear of the old house, the Link Building and the new house in 1753

eventually chosen was not illustrated until 1753 (by John Donowell). When the Sixth Duke of Devonshire laid out the Italian Garden further east, he unroofed the orangery, and used it as a trellis leading from one part of the garden to the other. It disappeared during the course of the nineteenth century.

Attributed to William Kent. One of a group of four proposals for a bridge and cascade, probably that at Chiswick, after 1727 but before 1743

The southern deer house was replaced in 1736 by the gateway whose inscription reveals that it was designed for Beaufort House, Chelsea, by the early seventeenth-century architect Inigo Jones. It was given to Lord Burlington by the later owner of that house, the famous collector and bibliophile Sir Hans Sloane.

Returning past the north front of the house, round its west side and into the forecourt, it is possible to gain access, via the Cascade at the south end of the so-called River, to the part of the garden developed after 1727.

Lord Burlington's additions after 1727

The last part of that development is the first to be reached. It is the Cascade, datable by a letter from William Kent to Lady Burlington, which describes it as unfinished in October 1738. Four proposal sketches in Kent's hand suggest that he may have been its architect.

The path over the top of the Cascade leads directly on to the Terrace made from the spoil excavated by forming what had hitherto been a straight canal into the present serpentine River. These works were made possible when Lord Burlington bought the estate on the west bank in 1727, but they were complete by 1728 when the terrace was described by the anonymous French tourist. The terrace was not a novelty: many sixteenth- and seventeenth-century English gardens had such raised walks along their boundaries, affording views over the wall. In this case it gave a view over water meadows and the Thames to the south. What was novel, however, was that it was planted naturalistically, with honeysuckles and roses on its south slope, and the ground to the north was laid out as a wilderness, with twisting walks and a circular clearing.

At the west end of the terrace a new entrance was formed from Burlington Lane, with an arched gate, and another *patte d'oie* centred on another obelisk. These were complete by 1733, when they were illustrated by Rigaud. The westerly avenue radiating from the *patte d'oie* was closed by the *Casina*, which was reached over a newly-constructed bridge. The central avenue was closed by the Ionic Temple, on to which a new, rear porch was attached.

Obelisks were, as explained above, although of Egyptian origin, considered to be of ancient Roman character. They, too, were of particular interest to the architects of sixteenth-century Rome. Peruzzi made a number of obelisk studies, and in the 1580s Pope Sixtus V embarked on a programme of re-erecting the obelisks of ancient Rome, which had all fallen. Obelisks on this scale had been introduced to England in 1702, by the architect Nicholas Hawksmoor, at Ripon, in Yorkshire, with the stated intention of producing an ancient Roman effect. The obelisk at the Burlington Lane gate made its ancient Roman intention explicit by the inclusion of a piece of real antique sculpture at its

Jacques Rigaud. The Casina, the rear of the Doric Temple and the east end of the Terrace, seen from the patte d'oie inside the Burlington Lane Gate in 1733. The Obelisk, in the foreground, incorporates one of the Arundel marbles.

Lewis Kennedy. The Conservatory, viewed from the south, with Kennedy's proposed Italian Garden in the foreground, 1814

base. This is the relief sculpture of a Roman wedding which, according to an anonymous writer in the *Gentleman's Magazine* in 1764, had once been part of the first collection of antique sculpture assembled in England, by the Earl of Arundel, a Jacobean courtier and patron of Inigo Jones. The relief was removed for safe-keeping in 1983, and is to be replaced by a copy.

Fifth Duke of Devonshire's changes, 1764–1811

The westerly exit from the Burlington Lane *patte d'oie* originally opened into a straight avenue leading to the *Casina*. But the Fifth Duke demolished the *Casina* in 1778, and his gardener, Samuel Lapidge, replaced the straight avenue with a serpentine carriage drive in 1784. It leads to the Stone Bridge, built in 1774, perhaps to the design of James Wyatt.

East of the River, in the area north of the Grove and west lawn, Lapidge swept away the two westerly avenues radiating from the *patte d'oie* and replaced them with a wilderness garden, traversed by a multiplicity of sinuous paths. Using any of these paths, a course struck out in a north-easterly direction leads eventually to the Rustic House (described above), in which Duchess Georgiana, the Fifth Duke's wife, placed a bust of Napoleon, whom she admired, although the country was then at war with him. It was made by the famous Danish neoclassical sculptor Thorwaldsen, and has recently been removed for safe-keeping. A cast will be put in its place.

Sixth Duke of Devonshire's additions, 1811–58

Napoleon's Walk, the path which leads south from the Rustic House, flanks the walled gardens. Bearing left towards the Doric Column, and, having passed that, turning left just before the Deer House, the west end of the Conservatory is reached. At this point the visitor crosses the boundary between land which belonged to Lord Burlington and land which was bought by the Sixth Duke of Devonshire in 1812.

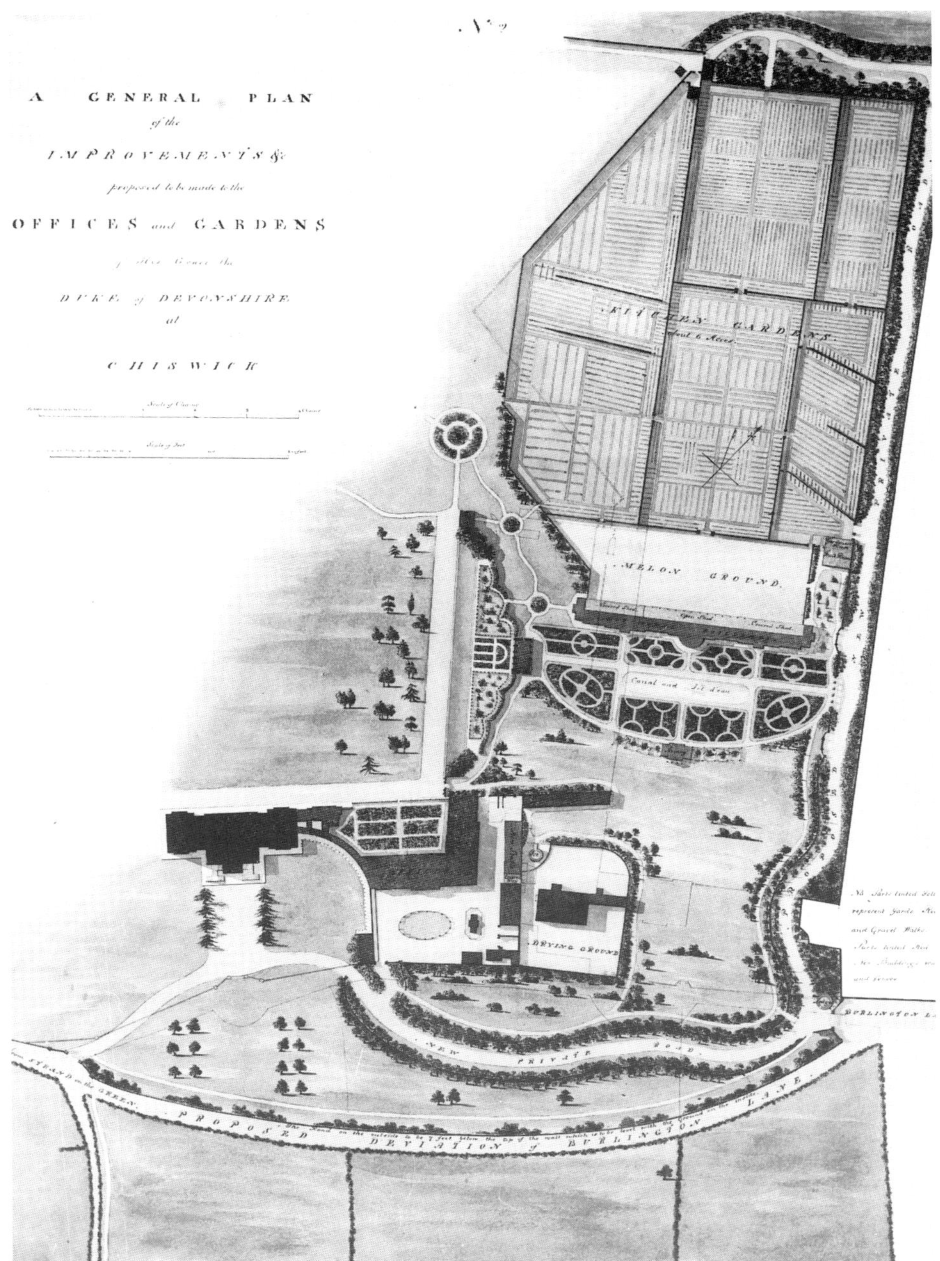

Lewis Kennedy. Proposal for laying out the additions to Chiswick House Gardens on the site of Moreton Hall and to the south of Burlington Lane, 1814

The Conservatory was designed by Samuel Ware and was complete by 1813. The main ranges at its east and west ends are of the glazed lean-to type relatively common in eighteenth-century kitchen gardens, although of a much bigger size than was usual. Its centre, however, has a semi-circular projection, and is roofed by a glazed dome (remodelled in 1933). This was more ambitious than most hot-houses, and was evidently the forerunner of the glazed domes designed by Decimus Burton at Kew and Paxton at Chatsworth, and of Paxton's masterpiece, the Crystal Palace. South of the Conservatory the Duke's gardener, Lewis Kennedy, laid out the Italian Garden, a parterre of complex geometrical design, filled with bedding-out plants. Either side of its central path stand two urns made in the artificial stone patented by the Lambeth firm of Coade and Seeley.

The Italian Garden can be left on its eastern side by a short path which leads at right angles into Duke's Avenue, an approach drive made by the Sixth Duke of Devonshire in 1821 from a new entrance at the northern extremity of his estate. At the south end of Duke's Avenue is the other entrance he made, from Burlington Lane, with piers copied from Lord Burlington's forecourt piers of 1727–29, and the lodge (known as Corney Road Lodge) added in 1835 to Decimus Burton's design. In 1813 the Duke also bought a strip of land south of the then alignment of Burlington Lane, and diverted the lane in a semi-circle further south. He made a new drive which can be followed from Corney Road Lodge westwards. It reaches the forecourt on the latter's east side, but the Duke extended the forecourt to nearly three times its original length in the form of an avenue of cedars, reaching to the new alignment of Burlington Lane. He moved the statuary from the forecourt, spreading it out along his new avenue. The avenue ended in a blind wall along the road, but in 1934 this was pierced by the insertion of a set of nineteenth-century gates and gate-piers from the demolished Grosvenor House, Park Lane. In 1950 Lord Burlington's forecourt was reconstructed, and the statuary returned to its original position.

HISTORY OF CHISWICK HOUSE AND GARDENS

Third Earl of Burlington

Lord Burlington was born in 1694, heir to one of the richest Anglo-Irish dynasties. His great-great-grandfather, the 'Great' Earl of Cork, had acquired a huge landholding in south-west Ireland during the reign of Charles I. The Second Earl of Cork married the heiress of the last Clifford Earl of Cumberland, from whom he inherited the Clifford estates in Westmorland and Yorkshire, and in recognition of this he was also created Earl of Burlington in 1664. Burlington is an ancient spelling of Bridlington (in Yorkshire) and since English peerages, unlike Irish ones, conferred a seat in the House of Lords, the family henceforth put the English earldom before the Irish one, despite the latter's seniority. In 1721 Lord Burlington himself married an heiress, Lady Dorothy Savile, daughter of the Second Marquess of Halifax, who brought him further estates in Yorkshire. Their patrimony is commemorated in the names of the streets he laid out behind his town house in Piccadilly: Cork Street, Clifford Street and Savile Row.

He succeeded to his titles at the age of ten, and came of age in 1715. He was a Whig and thus a supporter of the new Hanoverian king, George I, who appointed him Lord Treasurer of Ireland, Lord Lieutenant of both the East and West Ridings of Yorkshire, and Vice-Admiral of the County of York. He supported the Whig administration of Sir Robert Walpole from 1721, and was also a friend of the Prince of Wales and of his intelligent and cultured wife, the former Princess Caroline of Anspach. When the Prince succeeded as George II in 1727, Lord Burlington therefore enjoyed for six years a position close to the centre of power. His wife became Lady-in-Waiting to Queen Caroline, and in 1729 he was appointed a Privy Councillor. In May 1732, however, he opposed Walpole over the Excise Bill, along with Lords Chesterfield and Cobham. He resigned all his offices, and moved all his best pictures from his town house to Chiswick, which henceforth became his principal residence.

It had been in May 1714, at the age of 20, that Lord Burlington set off on his first Grand Tour, spending the three summer months in the Low Countries and the Rhineland, four autumn and winter months in Rome (during the first three of which he was ill, and confined to his chambers), and one month (April 1715) in Paris, on the return journey. In Rome he bought pictures, porphyry vases and musical instruments. He also brought back the sculptor Giovanni Battista Guelfi and the violinist Pietro Castrucci. His journey reveals no clear interest in architecture, nor partiality for a particular style, unless the long stay in Rome indicates an interest in classical antiquity.

In the summer of 1719, aged 25, he made a second tour, this time of only four months' duration and more specifically directed. For he had in the meantime come under the influence of two architectural books, published in 1715. One was the first English translation of the architectural theory and published designs of the sixteenth-century Venetian architect Andrea Palladio, produced by an architect of Venetian origin, James (or Giacomo) Leoni. The other was the compendium of the best of British classical architecture, made by an architect of Scottish origin,

Colen Campbell, who also claimed to be indebted to Palladio. Lord Burlington showed some favour to Leoni, and actually employed Campbell to design a new front to Burlington House in Piccadilly. Thus the 1719 tour was directed to Vicenza, Venice and their hinterland, the cities in which Palladio had spent his working life. But he also visited Genoa, where he admired palaces by Galeazzo Alessi (1512–72), and he may have visited the towns between there and Venice. This time he returned not merely with pictures, but with two collections of Palladio's architectural drawings, including the studies Palladio had made of Roman baths. He also brought back the painter William Kent and the composer Buononcini.

At an early age he became an architectural patron. From 1713 he began improving Londesborough Hall, his country seat in Yorkshire, using the local architect William Etty of York.

Between his two tours he had begun to embellish the façade of his London town house. This house (Burlington House) still stands, greatly enlarged and now housing the Royal Academy of Arts and the learned societies, on the north side of Piccadilly. His architects here were first James Gibbs, and then Colen Campbell. The new façade was begun in 1719, and some indication of Lord Burlington's eagerness to visit Vicenza and Venice is given by the fact that he set out on this tour while his new façade was under construction. Campbell claimed Palladio as the inspiration for his designs, although all the motifs he designed for Burlington House were actually taken from the master of seventeenth-century English classical architecture, Inigo Jones.

When Lord Burlington began to build his new house at Chiswick it was these two masters, Palladio and Jones, whom he elected as the presiding *genii* of the place. Their statues flank its entrance.

Building of the House

The property at Chiswick had been bought by the First Earl of Burlington in 1682. On it stood a mid seventeenth-century house, which survived until it was pulled down in 1788. Its site was just south-east of the present house, with which it was eventually linked. Lord Burlington, the Third Earl, re-designed the front elevation of its central range. Although a proposal drawing survives among his collection of architectural drawings, it is not possible to tell whether this work on the villa was carried out before or after Chiswick House was built. It was, however, complete by 1728, when it was illustrated in a view of the whole property by Pieter Andreas Rysbrack.

Lord Burlington was paying for work at Chiswick from at least 1719. His architect then was Colen Campbell, who came down to settle problems at least twice, and the clerk of works seems to have been John Simmons, a London joiner who laid out the houses on the east side of Grosvenor Square, with which Campbell was also concerned. This work may have been to the old house, or, more likely, to the garden buildings.

The present Chiswick House was almost certainly not begun before 1724, when it was conspicuous by its absence from John Macky's *Journey through England*, a travel book whose later editions, by contrast, describe the then new house. The design stage was under way in 1726, the date of a memo on which the design for the coffering of the cupola was sketched. The design was complete by 1727, when the building was published, almost as it is today, in William Kent's *Designs of Inigo Jones*. In the same year a visiting Scottish connoisseur, Sir John Clerk of Penicuik, reported Lord Burlington to be 'building a house . . . rather curious than convenient.' Lord Burlington's surviving accounts suggest that construction could have taken place either in 1722–24 or in 1727–29, but not in between. The interior was certainly being fitted out in the latter period, for the overmantels in the Red Velvet Room bear the date 1729. 1727–29 seems therefore to be the most likely construction period.

The understanding of Chiswick House has always been beset by uncertain knowledge of its intended function. It was once believed to be intended only for contemplation, conversation or entertainment, a sort of private gallery, library or club. This theory is supported by the observations made by contemporaries such as Sir John Clerk of Penicuik on its impracticability. Lord Hervey, for instance, described it as 'too little to live in, and too large to hang to one's watch'. It is supported also by the evidence both of the house itself and of the inventories of its contents, which show that it had a wine cellar, but no kitchen. And Horace Walpole, in 1760, wrote that the Eating Room was in the old house. On the other hand the inventory of 1770 reveals all the domestic requisites save a kitchen, including beds and bed linen. And Lady Burlington died in her bedchamber (in the south-east corner) in 1758. Small and inconvenient as it may have been, it must have been intended as a functioning house, even if the food had to be prepared and consumed in the old house adjoining.

Even so its relationship with the latter was most unusual. Lord Burlington could perhaps have intended to pull the old house down, leaving the new house, free-standing, as its replacement. He could have intended to pull the old house down, build a more appropriate replacement on its site, together with a wing on its further side duplicating the new house. He could have intended to use the new house as the centre of a larger house with flanking wings, as was actually done by his successor in 1788. But none of these seems likely in view of the fact that he spent money improving the old house before 1728. What he originally intended is not known. But what he eventually did was to link the two houses by a short gallery (known as the Link Building) on the garden front, connecting with a loggia (now destroyed) at right angles to it, which in turn led into the old house. That the link was an afterthought can be shown from the plan of its construction, which illustrates it in a different colour from the other buildings, indicating it to be a proposed addition. When the afterthought occurred cannot be precisely determined. But the Link Building is not shown on a view of the north front by Pieter Andreas Rysbrack datable to 1728 or 1729, nor on the plan of the new house published in William Kent's *Designs of Inigo Jones* in 1727. It is, however, shown in a view of the house by Rigaud datable to 1733. Its construction might account for the sudden rise in his expenditure on building between August and October 1732 (peaking at £1716 in September). And the need to create an enlarged house by linking the old and the new might have arisen by Lord Burlington's opposition to the Excise Bill in 1732–33 and the consequent removal of his principal possessions to Chiswick in 1733.

It is possible that the free-standing room east of the Link Building, known as the Summer Parlour, was added still later. There is a case for dating either the fitting out of this room, or its re-fitting, to 1735, as follows. The 1770 inventory records that the walls were hung with green silk damask. On 26 April 1735 Lady Burlington wrote to Lord Burlington about her 'branch' (meaning chandelier), requesting that 'the poize to be covered with Green silk of the same colour as the room.' Arguably this might refer to the Green Velvet Room. But the letter goes on to mention two commodes bearing Lady

Jacques Rigaud, Chiswick House, the Link Building, the Loggia, the old house and stable wing, seen

Burlington's owl badges, which were probably in the Summer Parlour. And a receipt from the upholsterer Stephen Langley for a set of 12 very expensive giltwood elbow chairs, which have been identified as for this room, is dated 11 April 1735.

The new house, the improvements to the old house, and the Link Building were all designed by Lord Burlington himself.

rom south of Burlington Lane in 1733

Although Lord Burlington employed draughtsmen, his designs were of his own invention. The first draughtsman, Samuel Savill (who died and was buried at Chiswick in 1728), was apparently used only for sketching details of which Lord Burlington wanted a record, and for measuring. The second, Henry Flitcroft, originally apprenticed to the Chiswick joiner Thomas Morris, was apparently used mainly for preparing finished drawings for publication. These publications specifically credited Lord Burlington with the designs. So did contemporaries in letters and journals. A large number of architectural drawings survive which are apparently drawn by him, and some are even signed by him. A French traveller in 1728, describing him as 'amant extremement l'architecture', even identified the garden pavilion in which he sat at his drawing board.

There is a persistent tradition, dating back no further than to an inaccurate history of 1845, that William Kent designed the interiors. There is no stylistic evidence for this, nor is there a documented payment to William Kent for work of any kind on any of Lord Burlington's buildings. However, John Vardy's *Some Designs of Mr Inigo Jones and Mr William Kent*, published in 1744, illustrates the original chimney-piece in the Summer Parlour, entitled '. . . at Cheswick . . . W. Kent invt.' A letter sent from Brian Fairfax to Lady Burlington in September 1735, at the time when she was paying for furniture for the Summer Parlour, makes it clear that Kent was then designing at least the interior of a room for her. So it is probable that the interior of the Summer Parlour was designed by Kent. The ceiling paintings are also attributed to Kent (whose letters describe how he painted ceilings for Lord Burlington at Burlington House), and, on the evidence of their style, this may be correct, for two of the pictorial innovations introduced by Kent are present at Chiswick. These are the grotesques in the ceilings of the Summer Parlour and Gallery, and the simulated mosaic backgrounds of the panels in the Blue Velvet Room.

Although other craftsmen in Lord Burlington's employment are known from his account books, it is not always possible to tell which building they worked on, as the recorded payments do not specify what work was done. But among those who received some payments for work at Chiswick were the bricklayer Richard Wright, the carpenter and joiner Thomas Morris, the joiner Thomas Board (who died before February 1722), the carpenter Thomas Peters (Board's executor), the plumber Robert Bourne, the glazier John Kent, the smith Thomas Kerton (whose business was later run by his widow Mary), the slater Evan Thomas, and the brazier Thomas Lincoln. Board (and therefore probably Peters too) and Kerton were Chiswick residents, and Lincoln came from Brentford.

Formation of the Garden

Phase I: before 1707

The garden which Lord Burlington inherited was clearly illustrated by Knyff and Kip in 1707. It surrounded the old house, which stood immediately east of the present forecourt. The road was nearer to the house than it is today, just south of the forecourt, and east of the old house there was a long range of office buildings with a stable yard between them and the road. The pleasure gardens proper were in three parts. Most ornamental of the three was a knot garden immediately north of the house and office range. West of the house, on the site of the present house and its forecourt, was a grass lawn subdivided into eight squares, each with a statue in the middle. North of both of these parts was a large walled enclosure divided by a tree-lined walk running from north to south. That walk, which, if extended south, would have passed along the west front of the old house, is the only one of these features to survive today. Around the pleasure gardens were productive gardens. Along the west side, reaching down to a tidal creek of the Thames known as the

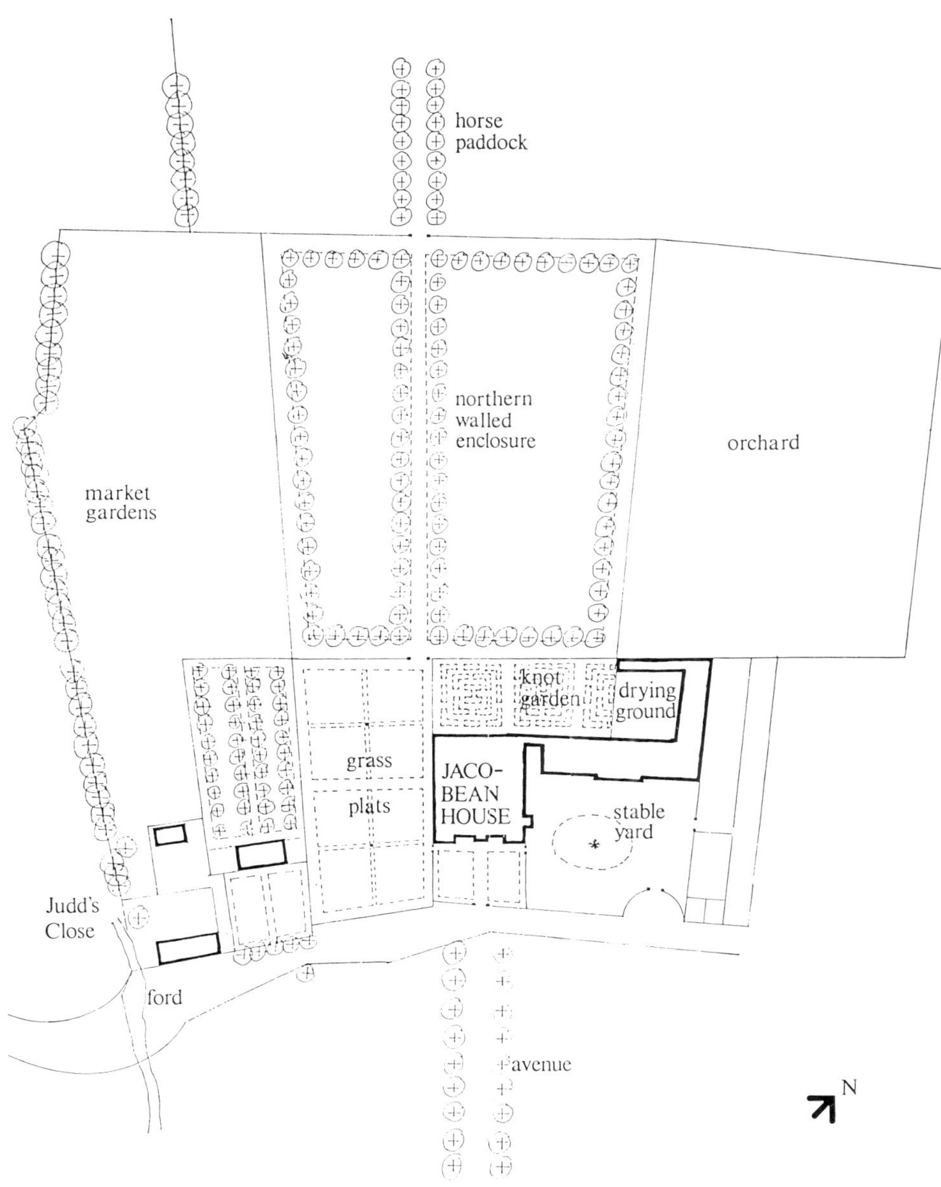

The gardens of old Chiswick House in 1707

Pieter Andreas Rysbrack. The Bollo Brook, northern pond and Tuscan pavilion, c *1728*

Bollo Brook, was a vegetable garden. To the east was an orchard. To the north was a paddock.

Phase II: after 1707, and before 1717 (probably) or 1727 (certainly)

The first of Lord Burlington's changes can only be dated very imprecisely. It was definitely complete by *c* 1727–28 (when a new phase began), for one of the buildings he added (the Ionic Temple) was illustrated in William Kent's *Designs of Inigo Jones*, published in 1727, a French tourist described the improvements as he saw them in 1728, and the Flemish artist Pieter Andreas Rysbrack made some paintings of them in that year (two of which hang in the Blue Velvet Room). It was probably complete ten years earlier. Certainly one of the buildings Lord Burlington added was illustrated in Colen Campbell's *Vitruvius Britannicus*, published in 1717, Pope asked to show visitors round in 1719 (suggesting completion), and Lord Burlington's accounts show no substantial expenditure on gardening after 1719 until the next phase began in 1727.

The improvements consisted principally of extensions. The former paddock to the north was made into a wilderness garden, subdivided by avenues as follows. At the north end of the tree-lined walk which divided the walled enclosure, Lord Burlington made what contemporary gardeners called a *patte d'oie* (French for goose's foot). This was the meeting point of three radiating avenues lined with tall hedges. Each one ended in a small building. The western one ended with the *Casina*, sometimes referred to as the *Bagnio*, which backed on to the Bollo Brook. It was illustrated in *Vitruvius Britannicus*, in 1717, which specifically described it as having been designed by Lord Burlington. The central avenue ended with the Pagan Temple, a building which appears to have been in the style of Gibbs. The easterly avenue ended in the Rustic House, which is designed in a style

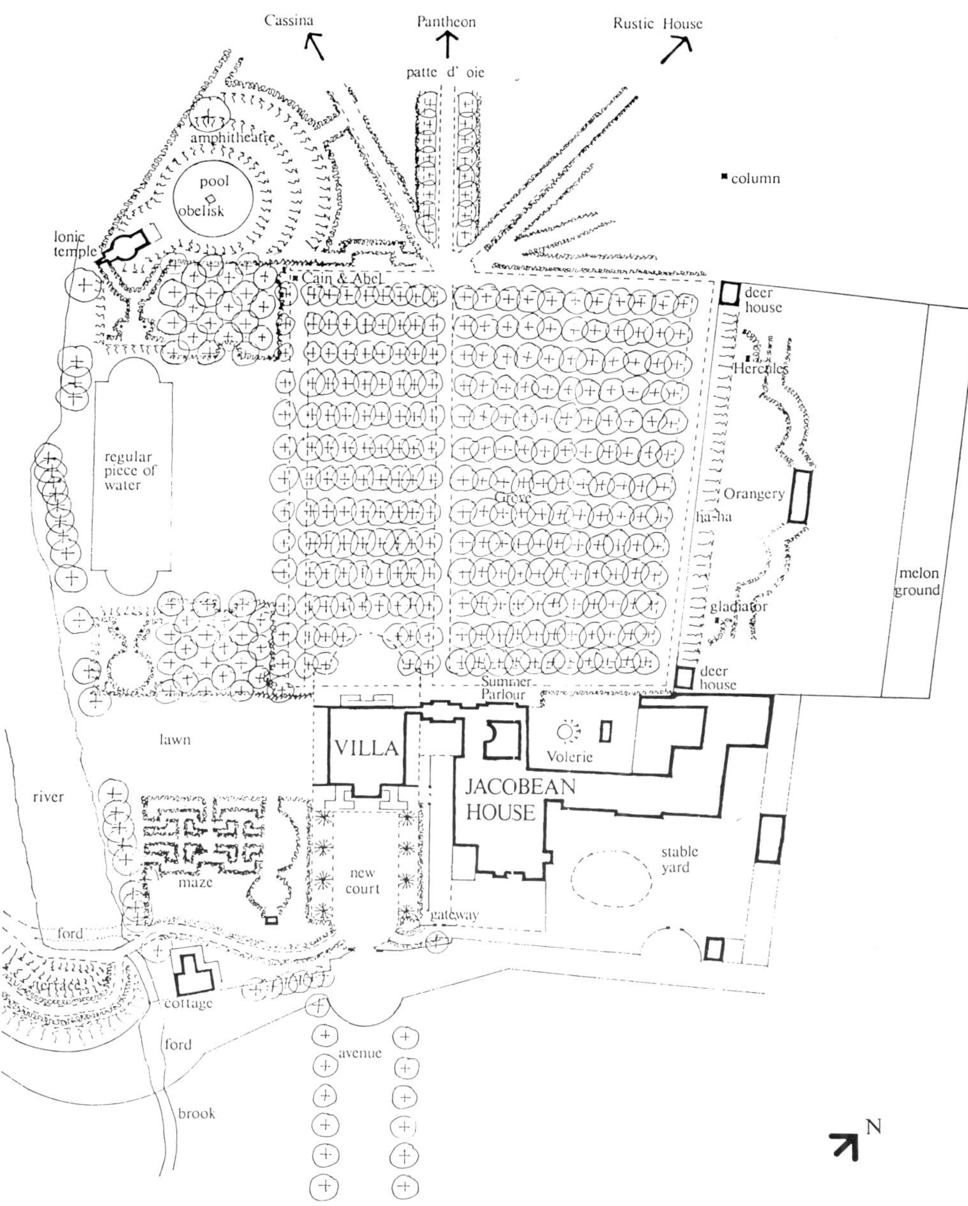

The gardens of Chiswick House in 1733

compatible with either Campbell's or Lord Burlington's. Of these three buildings, only the Rustic House survives. South-east of the easterly avenue a short subsidiary avenue was formed, leading to a free-standing Doric column with a statue after the Venus de Medici on top. Between the westerly avenue and the Bollo Brook, Lord Burlington excavated a grass amphitheatre surrounding a circular pool in which stood an obelisk. On the steps of the amphitheatre, orange trees were placed in tubs. Behind the pool stood an Ionic temple, modelled on the Pantheon in Rome, backing on to the Bollo Brook. The temple was illustrated in William Kent's *Designs of Inigo Jones* (1727), where Lord Burlington is described as the architect. Amphitheatre, pool, obelisk and temple, all survive today. To their north, between them and the Casina, but still west of the westerly avenue, a rectangular piece of water was formed, with sloping grass banks and semi-circular ends. On its east side a brick pavilion was built, with a Tuscan portico derived from Inigo Jones's church of St Paul, Covent Garden. On the water a rowing boat was kept. Water and pavilion were probably removed by Samuel Lapidge in 1784.

The kitchen garden to the west of the walled enclosure was also brought into the pleasure gardens. In its centre Lord Burlington formed another rectangular piece of water with sloping grass banks and semi-circular projections at each end. The spoil excavated from it was formed into mounds to north and south, planted with trees. It was filled in and the mounds levelled in 1772.

The orchard to the east of the walled enclosure was converted into a deer paddock, and the wall which separated it from the centre was replaced by a ha-ha (sunk fence) to keep the deer in the paddock. At the north and south of the ha-ha stood little deer houses, with doors on both their west and east sides. Only the ha-ha and the northern deer house survive today, the latter in a style compatible with either Campbell's or Lord Burlington's.

In the centre of all these improvements the walled enclosure was transformed into a Grove, losing its confining walls, and gaining trees closely planted at regular intervals. At its north-west corner stood a lead group of Samson slaying the Philistine, moved to Chatsworth in 1928.

Phase III: after 1727, and before 1733

In 1727 Lord Burlington bought Sutton Court, the estate on the west bank of the Bollo Brook, and laid out the part nearest to the house in a form recorded in drawings by the French artist Jacques Rigaud, dated 1733.

The Bollo Brook, whose banks had been cut to form it into a straight canal, was made irregular at its south end, and greatly enlarged at its north end. The spoil excavated in doing so was formed into a raised terrace to border the southern edge of the newly acquired addition, and given views southwards across the meadows to the Thames. In 1738 Defoe described how it was formed, but a French tourist mentioned its existence ten years earlier, and that in turn means that the Bollo Brook must have been excavated by then. One of Pieter Andreas Rysbrack's paintings of 1728 is a view north from the top of the terrace, and it also shows the newly acquired property being transformed into a wilderness garden, with a circular clearing in the angle between the terrace and the 'River', as the Bollo Brook now became. By 1733 Rigaud's view shows that this clearing housed another circular pond. The River and terrace survive today, but not the pond or its clearing.

At the west end of the terrace an arched gate was built. Inside was a circular clearing with an obelisk incorporating at its base an antique relief sculpture. An

Jacques Rigaud. The Terrace, western Wilderness Garden and Bollo Brook, from the south in 1733

anonymous article in the *Gentleman's Magazine* in 1764 identifies this sculpture as having once formed part of the collection made by the Earl of Arundel, a famous Jacobean collector and patron of Inigo Jones. The circular clearing was the basis of another *patte d'oie* with three radiating avenues. The eastern one ran below the north side of the terrace to a ford through the River, and thence by a serpentine route up to the house. The central one was aligned on the rear of the Ionic Temple, on the eastern side of the river. A porch was added on the west (rear) side of the Ionic Temple, to face down this avenue. The northern avenue was aligned on the *Casina*, and crossed the river by means of a bridge. These works were all completed by 1733, when they were illustrated by the French artist Jacques Rigaud. The bridge and ford are even shown, with a carriage splashing through the latter, on Pieter Andreas Rysbrack's paintings of 1728. As they are all part of the same scheme, they were probably all executed together, at the earlier date, by 1728. The arched gate, the obelisk and the porch on the rear of the Ionic temple all survive today. But the ford was replaced by the Cascade in 1738, and the bridge by a bigger bridge in 1774.

From the bridge radiated another *patte d'oie*, facing westwards, with avenues reaching out over the rest of the former Sutton Court property, which Lord Burlington laid out as a park. He stocked it with deer from Londesborough, and doubtless also moved the deer from the paddock on the east side, freeing that for further developments.

Meanwhile, probably between 1727 and 1729, he had built the new house on the site of the former lawn, and that required some adjustments to the garden immediately adjacent. The southern part of the lawn became the forecourt to the new house, its southern end semi-circular, and pierced by three gates, the central one to the road, the eastern one leading to the front of the old house, and the western one leading down to the ford. The southern end of the former kitchen garden became a lawn falling from the west side of the new house down to the river, and on its south side a maze was planted. Where the trees of the Grove came too close to the north front of the house a semi-circular clearing was formed, and demarcated by an iron railing. These were recorded in Pieter Andreas Rysbrack's paintings, done about the same time. All survive today, except for the railing and the maze which were swept away by the time George Lambert painted the house in 1742.

Phase IV : after 1733, and before 1753
Three contemporaries, Horace Walpole, Sir Thomas Robinson and Joseph Spence, wrote independently that in 1733–34 Lord Burlington and Kent had introduced 'the natural taste in gardening'. Spence, writing 24 years later, went so far as to specify the month, October 1733, when this taste was introduced to Chiswick. He could not decide which of the two was responsible, but Walpole was certain that it was Kent who 'first leaped the fence and saw that all nature was a garden'. It is difficult to ignore the evidence of such well-informed critics as these three, but it must also be said, first, that nothing but sketches survive in William Kent's hand, sketches which are as often records as proposals, and, second, that the style of the works undertaken after 1733 does not differ from that of the earlier works, except in one important area.

This area was that immediately west of the new house. Already a sloping lawn fell towards the River. Between the making of Rocque's map in 1736 and a painting by George Lambert dated 1742, this lawn was enlarged by grubbing up the maze to its south. Instead of providing a straight-sided and confined view of the River, the expanded lawn brought the house and the irregularly shaped water into a unified

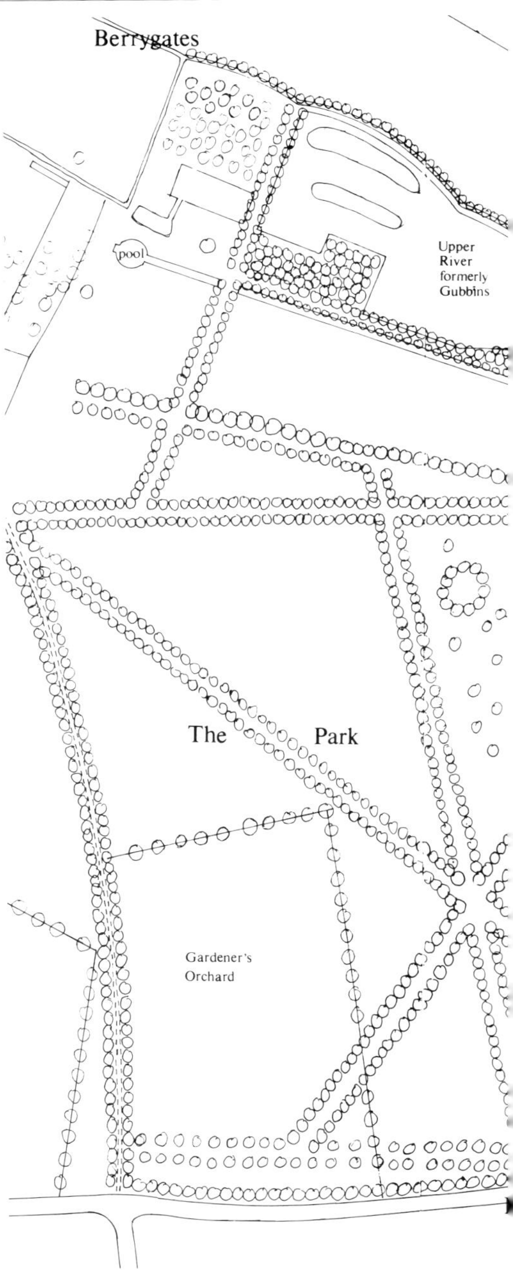

The gardens of Chiswick House in 1753

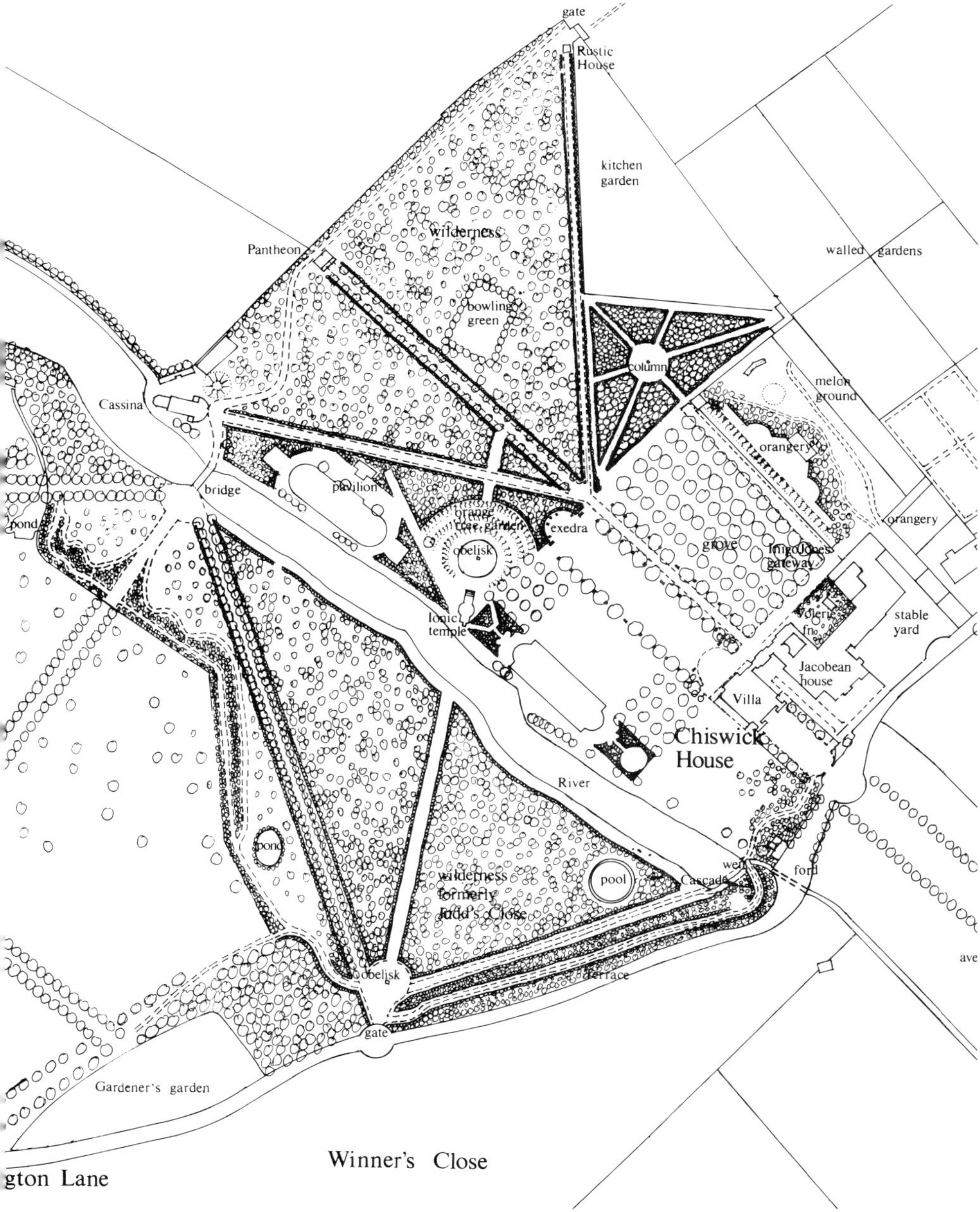

gate
Rustic House
kitchen garden
wilderness
Pantheon
walled gardens
bowling green
column
melon ground
Cassina
orangery
bridge
pavilion
orange tree garden
exedra
orangery
pond
obelisk
grove
Inigo Jones gateway
Ionic temple
volerie
fn.
stable yard
Jacobean house
Villa
Chiswick House
River
pond
well
ford
pool
Cascade
wilderness formerly Judd's Close
ave
obelisk
Terrace
gate
Gardener's garden
Winner's Close
gton Lane

Pieter Andreas Rysbrack (detail). The rear elevation of the Casina with the bridge to its right, seen from the north end of the Bollo Brook, c *1728*

visual relationship. This relationship, which later became a type of the landscape garden, was undoubtedly the novelty that Walpole, Robinson and Spence identify it as. But, as is appropriate to a pioneering venture, at Chiswick it was both modest in scale, and limited to one part of the garden, which was otherwise developed in the same style as before.

The second group of works of the period 1733–36 were also a consequence of the building of the new house. On the north front the formation of a semi-circular clearing in the Grove proved to be not enough, and a swath was cleared through the Grove the full width of the new house. Its north end terminated in a semi-circle of yew with niches cut for the three Roman statues formerly placed in Ionic Temple, alternating with four large stone urns. The germ of this idea may well have been Kent's, for a sketch in his hand survives, showing the semi-circle executed in stone, which must therefore be a proposal rather than a record. Furthermore Kent designed something similar at Stowe and at Rousham. This arrangement, called the *exedra*, was not begun in 1733 when Rigaud made his views, but was complete by 1736, when it appears on Rocque's map, and it survives today.

Further opening up of the area north of the house took place between Rocque's map and Donowell's engravings of 1753. During this time the remaining trees in the western half of the Grove were felled, opening up a view to the rectangular pond, and the River beyond. The *exedra* was linked to the house by two lines of statuary. These consisted of a wolf and a boar, carved by the statuary Peter Scheemakers, at the south end, two lions at the north end, and two rows of urns in between, alternating with cypress trees, and interrupted in the middle by two stone sphinxes. As the eastern line of urns flanked what had been the central pathway across the Grove, it was evidently felt necessary also to provide another row of urns on the other (eastern) side of this path. A lead sphinx made by the sculptor John Cheere was added later to this row of urns in 1748.

The third group of works of the period 1733–36 was presumably consequent on the creation of the deer park on the Sutton Court property. As the deer pasture to the east thereby became available, it was decided to turn it into an orange tree garden with an orangery on its eastern side, flanked by hedges. Lord Burlington made several designs for an orangery. One was evidently under consideration in 1733 when it was illustrated by Rigaud, another in 1736 when it was illustrated by Rocque, but the one which was built is shown by Donowell existing in 1753. It was unroofed soon after 1814, and used as a trellis. There was also no need for the deerhouses, and when, in 1736, Lord Burlington was offered Inigo Jones' gateway from Beaufort House, Chelsea, he put it on the site of the south deerhouse. It still survives.

South of the ford, Lord Burlington intended a cascade composed of rockwork like the grottoes of the sixteenth century he had seen in Italy. Both he and Kent appear to have prepared designs.

One is illustrated on Rocque's map of 1736, and it might therefore be presumed complete by that date were it not for a letter from Kent to Lady Burlington saying that it was unfinished in October 1738. In 1742 Defoe described it as having failed. In 1746 Lord Burlington spent £182 trying to make it work. Its final form is shown in a view by John Donowell dated 1753. It survives in a form altered by the Sixth Duke of Devonshire.

Character of Lord Burlington's Architecture and Garden Design

Lord Burlington's principal objective was to re-create the architecture and gardens of ancient Rome. He was not content just to reproduce its appearance. He wished also to re-establish its meaning. His buildings and gardens incorporated sculpture or painted ornament which told a story or pointed a moral. Burlington House, for instance, was decorated to illustrate chastity, faithful love and marital fidelity. Chiswick House incorporates an allegorical exposition of the polite arts. Its garden includes references to political liberty.

Information about Roman buildings and gardens was not as abundant as he could have wished. So Lord Burlington was dependent on an earlier generation who had attempted the same task. These were the architects of sixteenth-century Italy, especially Rome, whom historians now call Mannerists. Their names are Raphael (1643–1520), Baldassare Peruzzi (1486–1536), Giulio Romano (1499–1546), Giacomo Vignola (1507–1573) and Pirro Ligorio (1510–1583). He was also influenced by their north Italian contemporaries, Galeazzo Alessi (1512–1572) in Genoa, and Andrea Palladio (1508–1580) in Vicenza and Venice. Palladio was of especial importance to Lord Burlington as he had published a book of his own designs, which included most of the features pioneered by the Roman Mannerists. The only British architect who had set himself similar objectives was the pioneering English classicist Inigo Jones (1573–1652). All these architects were entranced by the mythic and poetic aspects of ancient culture, and they designed buildings which were intended to be meaningful and allusive.

The gravity with which these earlier architects had approached the task of exposing an ancient and superior culture is less apparent in the work of Lord Burlington. His correspondence reveals a degree of humour in his personal relationships, which in turn invests his designs with a quality of Arcadian levity. This is one of the characteristics of his own age, nowadays known as the Rococo period. The gardens at Chiswick, for instance, had buildings like the Rustic House or the Pagan Temple, whose meanings cannot possibly have been intended to be taken seriously. The gardens are divided into compartments, each relatively small, and they are contrived with a degree of artifice which was repugnant to the naturalistic school of the next generation. These, too, were Rococo characteristics.

Influence and Importance of Lord Burlington

The allusive nature of Lord Burlington's architecture is partly explained by his interests in the other arts, besides architecture. In fact he was the most considerable patron of the arts and of scholarship in Georgian England. His name appears on the subscription lists of 154 books: only the second Earl of Oxford and Sir Hans Sloane, whose libraries formed the nucleus of the British Museum, subscribed to more. He supported, among others, the philosopher Berkeley, the writers Pope, Swift, Gay and Thomson, the musician Handel and his rival Buononcini, the librettists Haym and Rolli, the painter and architect Kent, and the sculptors Guelfi and Rysbrack. Gay, Handel, Kent and Guelfi, at different times, actually lived under his roof at Burlington House in Piccadilly, and William Kent apparently occupied an intimate place in the life and affections of his family. And Lady Burlington provided a dowry for the dancer Violetti on her marriage to Garrick.

Music was the Burlingtons' second interest, perhaps inherited from his mother, to whom Heidegger dedicated the libretto of the opera *Antiochus* in 1711. Handel first became Lord Burlington's guest in 1712, when the latter was only eighteen. In 1715 Lord Burlington brought back from Italy the cellist and composer Filippo Amadei, and the violinists Pietro and Prospero Castrucci. In 1719 he returned with the composer Giovanni Buononcini, and was responsible for his initial collaboration with Handel. In 1719 he was the principal promoter of the Royal Academy of Music, and, when that failed, he became, in 1733, one of the principal promoters of the short-lived Opera of the Nobility. Opera was his particular musical interest, and that is reflected in his collection of drawings, of which one third were stage designs.

Lord Burlington's influence on architecture was more successful. During the period of his influence at court he managed to obtain posts in the Office of Works (the government building department) for his own protégés. The Hon Richard Arundell, Lord Burlington's executor, and, one might therefore presume, his closest intimate, became Surveyor General of the King's Works (chief government architect) in 1726. William Kent became Master Carpenter in 1726, Master Mason and Deputy Surveyor in 1735. Henry Flitcroft became Clerk of Works at Whitehall, Westminster and St James in 1726, Master Carpenter in 1746, Master Mason and Deputy Surveyor on Kent's death in 1748, and Comptroller in 1758 (although Flitcroft may also have been aided by family connections of his own within the Works establishment). These men continued to hold their posts after Lord Burlington's resignation, and no doubt their tenure of office enabled him to resign confident that his influence would be maintained. Flitcroft held his posts until his death in 1769, having trained up an assistant, Kenton Couse, who continued the Burlington style until 1790.

In addition Lord Burlington's social position enabled him to introduce his protégés to private clients. Kent obtained the best private commissions of the time, working for the Queen, the Prince of Wales, four Dukes, two Prime Ministers, and other leading politicians. Flitcroft developed a private practice which enabled him to buy an estate in Hampstead and lead the life of a gentleman in the house that he built there. Other architects whom Lord Burlington favoured gained introductions to his social circle: Leoni, for instance, was employed by five members of the Boyle family alone.

His influence also extended by example. Burlington House was prominently located in London's most fashionable quarter. It was one of London's largest houses, the only one with a stone façade, and the most lavishly ornamented. Behind it he laid out an entire estate of fashionable houses, two of which were designed by him, one by Kent, four by Campbell, one by Campbell's assistant Roger Morris, and two by Leoni. Chiswick was located in an area where the leading courtiers either built themselves suburban retreats, or wished to do so, and, among these, it was the most striking. In 1736, in Lord Burlington's absence, it was visited by Queen Caroline and her daughters, purely as a spectacle, with Kent as their guide. It was described directly by the writers Defoe and Macky, and obliquely, as an example, by Pope. Pope's recurrent advocation of Burlington's architectural style and his *Epistle to Lord Burlington* were unchallenged in the literary and intellectual world. In this world, his reputation also spread by word of mouth, reaching Berlin, where in 1751 Frederick the Great asked the Italian philosopher Algarotti to show him pictures of Lord Burlington's work.

Few of those influenced by him deployed the style of Lord Burlington with genius. The others applied his favoured ornament to buildings of a more traditional character. But in the 1760s another architect whose style had been refreshed by prolonged study of Roman antiquities took London by storm. This was Robert Adam, and his buildings were influenced not just by Lord Burlington's ornament, but by his elevations and plans as well. Adam published his own designs, which were extremely influential, as much in France as in England. There were few architects of the neoclassical period who did not learn something from Adam, and thus, indirectly from Lord Burlington. It could therefore be said that Lord Burlington's importance consists in being a pioneer of neoclassical architecture.

Later history of the house

On Lord Burlington's death in 1753 his estates passed to the Marquess of Hartington, the husband of his only surviving daughter, Charlotte. Lord Hartington succeeded as Fourth Duke of Devonshire in 1755, and thereafter Chiswick belonged to successive Dukes of Devonshire until 1929.

The Fourth Duke died in 1764, and the Fifth Duke resided little at Chiswick until the 1790s. The Fourth Duke's favourite architect was James Paine, and the Fifth Duke's was, at first, John Carr. But when the Fifth Duke turned his attention to Chiswick, he engaged the services of John White, hitherto surveyor to the Portland estate in Marylebone, who subsequently succeeded Carr as the Duke's architect at Buxton, building there one minor masterpiece, the neoclassical church of St

John Buckler. Chiswick House, with flanking wings, in 1822

John, in 1811–13.

The Duke decided to rationalise the illogicalities surviving from Lord Burlington's arrangement of 1727–29, and to complete the process which the latter had begun *c*1732 of transforming the new house into a properly serviced country seat. In 1788 he pulled down the old house and the loggia, and White replaced them with flanking wings to the house of 1727–29. The east wing enveloped the Link Building of *c*1732. White also made some improvements to the office range. The masons were Robert Ashton and son, the bricklayer 'Sush' Wright, the slaters Ann Tyson and sons, the carpenter and joiner Thomas Hall, the plasterer John Papworth, the painter Thomas Hill, and the glazier Henry James. Lysons' *Environs of London* describes the wings as 'scarcely finished' in 1794. The house was now larger, better serviced, and bereft of the inconveniences on which Lord Burlington's contemporaries had commented.

The Fifth Duke's wife was the famous Duchess Georgiana, daughter of the First Earl Spencer, and the leading political hostess of the reforming Whig party. She was devoted to the Whig leader Charles James Fox who opposed the war with revolutionary France and admired Napoleon. To please Fox, she commissioned from the Danish sculptor Thorwaldsen, a bust of Napoleon, which was placed in the garden. The avenue leading up to it was renamed Napoleon's Walk. Fox died in the Duchess's care in Chiswick in 1806, in the Bedchamber.

The Fifth Duke died in 1811, and was succeeded by his son, known as the Bachelor Duke, who was to employ Wyattville to build the north wing at Chatsworth, but who is better known as the employer of Sir Joseph Paxton, designer of the Crystal Palace. At Chiswick his architect was Samuel Ware, but his activities seem to have been limited to garden buildings.

The Bachelor Duke made more use of the house than anyone since Lord Burlington, although the nature of his hospitality was not that of his forebear, a continued cultural discourse, but of near-official dignity and of princely cost. In 1814 he received Tsar Alexander I of Russia and King Frederick William III of Prussia at Chiswick, in 1842 he received Queen Victoria and Prince Albert, and in 1844 he laid on a spectacular entertainment for Tsar Nicholas I. On the latter occasion the Summer Parlour was decorated as a tent in the style of the fourteenth century, while at Chatsworth the Emperor Fountain (the highest in Europe) was built in the Tsar's honour, together with an aqueduct across the moors to supply it. The Duke was also a friend of the Prime Minister, George Canning, who died in a room in one of John White's wings, in 1827, while still in office.

The Bachelor Duke died in 1858, leaving Chiswick to his sister Lady Granville. On her death in 1862 it was let to a succession of tenants, including the Duchess of Sutherland in 1867, the Prince of Wales in the 1870s, and the Marquess of Bute, famous as the restorer of Castel Coch and the patron of William Burges, from 1881 to 1892. The Duchess of Sutherland maintained the liberal traditions of Duchess Georgiana, frequently entertaining Gladstone, and receiving Garibaldi at Chiswick on his visit to London. The Prince of Wales maintained the traditions of the Bachelor Duke, receiving the Shah of Persia at Chiswick in 1873. From 1892 to 1929 it was let as a private lunatic asylum.

In 1929 the estate was bought by Middlesex County Council to prevent the Ninth Duke from redeveloping it. The grounds were leased to the Urban District of Brentford and Chiswick, whose successor body, the London Borough of Hounslow, now own them. After the Second World War, the need for repairs to the house and the emerging recognition of its architectural importance resulted in its gift to the Minister of Works. The house was transferred to the care of the Historic Buildings and Monuments Commission for England (English Heritage) on the formation of that body in 1984.

Later history of the garden

The opening of the Grove between 1733 and 1743 did little to dispel the feeling, by late eighteenth-century standards, of artificiality. When Thomas Jefferson, in England to negotiate the Treaty of Paris, visited Chiswick in 1786, he noted 'the garden shows still too much of art'.

Yet some of Lord Burlington's art had even then been destroyed. The Fifth Duke of Devonshire had filled in the southern rectangular pond in 1772, pulled down the *Casina* in 1778, and the Pagan Temple by 1784. This is not evidence of neglect, for in 1774 he had rebuilt the Stone Bridge in its present splendid form, perhaps to the design of James Wyatt. Rather it was a change of taste, away from artificial temples located within a geometrically ordered plan. In 1784 the Duke engaged Samuel Lapidge, Capability Brown's former assistant and successor, to bring the gardens up to date. Lapidge planted out the east and west avenues of the *patte d'oie* in the western wilderness garden, and in place of the avenue from the Obelisk Gate to the Stone Bridge he laid out a serpentine carriage drive. In place of the two avenues from the northern *patte d'oie* to the sites of the *Casina* and Pagan Temple, he replanned the wilderness as a maze of sinuous paths. It may be that Lapidge also filled in the northern rectangular pond: it had certainly gone by 1818. These eliminations of art had mostly taken place by the time of Jefferson's visit.

In 1812 the Sixth Duke bought Moreton Hall, the neighbouring estate to the east, and pulled the house down. To the north of its site he built the Conservatory, designed by the architect Samuel Ware, and complete by 1813. Its east and west ranges are a hot-house of conventional design, with a glazed lean-to roof against a heated north wall, but its centre had a magnificent glazed dome. It is a forerunner of Decimus Burton's hot-house at Kew, and Sir Joseph Paxton's at Chatsworth (built for the Duke himself) and at the Crystal Palace. In 1828 the Duke filled it with an outstanding collection of camellias. South of the Conservatory the gardener Lewis Kennedy laid out an 'Italian Garden' in 1814. Taste having reverted since Samuel Lapidge's day towards formal planting plans, this was a semi-circle of geometrical parterres with Coade stone urns and bedding-out plants. Around the Doric Column he laid out a concentric rosery. The Conservatory (although altered in 1933) and the Italian Garden both survive today, but the rosery decayed in the nineteenth century.

Lord Burlington's Orangery was made redundant by the new Conservatory. The Sixth Duke therefore had its roof removed to form a pergola linking the old and new gardens. The little garden in front of it became a pheasantry. By 1824 the Duke also had golden and silver pheasants, and an elephant, which he probably kept on the north and west lawns. By 1825 he had a monkey and a cockatoo. By the time of the Tsar's visit in 1844, he also had a giraffe, elks, emus, kangaroos, an Indian bull and cow, goats and a Neapolitan pig.

The northern end of the Moreton Hall property was a walled garden, with magnificent iron gates on its south side, designed perhaps by Hugh May, architect of Moreton Hall in 1682. The Duke kept

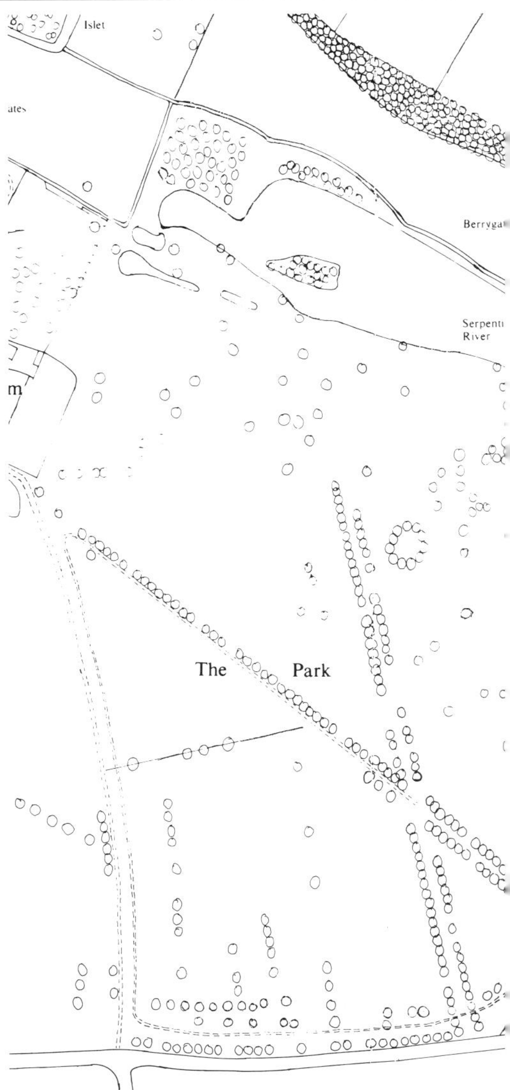

The gardens of Chiswick House in 1818

it, and laid out the centre of the Conservatory and the Italian Garden on its axis.

The Duke also decided to improve his access. In 1813 he bought a strip of land south of the road, and diverted the latter in

a semi-circle further south. He also bought a thin strip of land on the further (eastern) side of the Moreton Hall property, at the southern end of which Lewis Kennedy proposed a lodge, with a private drive from this lodge along the line of the old road to reach the forecourt from the east. The lodge (Corney Road Lodge) was eventually built to Decimus Burton's design in 1835, and still survives. Lewis Kennedy also proposed a serpentine drive from the highway at Turnham Green, winding round to approach the house from the west, but in 1821 the Duke decided to use the eastern strip of land, running a drive down it from the north to Corney Road Lodge. This, too, survives and is known as Duke's Avenue.

The park was sold off for building land by the Seventh Duke in 1884. His tenant, the Marquess of Bute, laid out a path from the north front of the house to an oval termination in place of the *exedra*, while removing the path to the *patte d'oie* which had originally divided the Grove. In 1950, shortly before the house was restored, this work was undone. The path reverted to its Georgian position, the *exedra* and the *patte d'oie* were replanted, and the two missing avenues from the *patte d'oie* were reconstructed in their pre-1784 form, although not exactly on their original alignments.

Restoration of 1956–57

Nineteenth-century popular taste regarded classical architecture as unremarkable. By the 1920s it was recognised as a diminishing commodity, and its masterpieces as truly precious. Two results of this change in taste were the public acquisition of Chiswick House and Park in 1929, and the formation of the Georgian Group in 1937. After the Second World War the Georgian Group pressed central government for a full restoration of Chiswick House.

Beside the growth of popular and professional interest in Georgian architecture, there was also a re-evaluation of Lord Burlington by art historians. In the nineteenth century he had been regarded as little more than an involved patron. The designs which had been published as his were assumed to have been ghosted by a draughtsman, usually said to be William Kent. But in 1927 the American scholar Fiske Kimball succeeded in establishing that Lord Burlington was a practising architect. In three articles written in 1945 and 1954, the German émigré art historian Rudolf Wittkower went further. Lord Burlington, he argued, was no ordinary architect, but a stylistic innovator. Wittkower gave Lord Burlington an architectural personality with three innovatory characteristics. These were, first, a tendency to compose his buildings in visually separate blocks, easy to distinguish but difficult to integrate. Wittkower described this compositional characteristic as having a *staccato* quality. Secondly, Lord Burlington designed buildings to resemble ancient Roman architecture in a more single-minded way than anyone previously, with but small regard for the convenience of their users. Thirdly, Lord Burlington derived from Palladio a system for proportioning the parts of his building in a manner which, although invisible to the casual onlooker, followed geometrical laws. These laws were those which aesthetic theorists, both in the ancient world and in Renaissance Italy, had believed governed not just geometry, but also music, architecture, and ultimately, the harmony and equilibrium of the entire universe.

The consequences of Wittkower's interpretation were far-reaching. In 1955 another German émigré scholar, Emil Kaufmann, published a book which argued that the crucial change which brought about a modern method of architectural composition came in the eighteenth century, when the previous system (which we now call Baroque) of integrating the individual parts of the composition with each other and subordinating them to a unified whole was gradually abandoned in favour of a system in which individual elements were clearly separated. Wittkower's identification of the *staccato* characteristic of Lord Burlington's

The Orange Tree Garden today. A painting of the garden c *1728 appears on page 29*

composition therefore made him a pioneer of modern design, according to Kaufmann's thesis.

About the same time the neoclassical style of architecture of *c* 1800, in which buildings were intended to resemble ancient Greek or Roman examples, began to be appreciated as never before. In a book of 1965, a Canadian scholar, Professor Peter Collins, even argued that all the theoretical explanations of modern architecture were first formulated in the neoclassical period. Wittkower's recognition that Lord Burlington was a pioneer of this style gave him a position of remarkable historical consequence, according to this view.

But, influential as were Kaufmann's and Collins's books, they were eclipsed by a book which had been written in 1948 by Wittkower himself, *Architectural Principles in the Age of Humanism*. Wittkower took the view that Renaissance architecture, instead of being an assemblage of pretty ornament devoid of meaning (which had made it detestable to Ruskin in the 1850s, and delightful to Geoffrey Scott in the 1920s), was ruled by a system of geometric laws, which themselves expressed, in a mathematical form, the harmony and balance of the universe. In Wittkower's book the finest practitioner of this type of composition was the Italian architect Palladio. In his articles on Lord Burlington he had already identified the latter as Palladio's principal English disciple.

No book written by a historian in modern times has had such an effect on practising architects. In 1947 the English architect Colin Rowe published an article entitled 'The Mathematics of the Ideal Villa', which claimed that Palladio and Le Corbusier designed buildings according to the same set of principles. So Palladio and, for English students, Lord Burlington were recognised as the first Modern Movement architects. At a time when, presumably under the influence of Mao Tse Tung, architectural history was being erased from the architectural schools, and when Reyner Banham, the leading historian of Modernism, was inviting students to 'shed their entire cultural load', these two unusually well-loaded architects were allowed to be the exception. At the Bartlett School of Architecture, one of the most progressive of the day, history was a forbidden subject, except for two carefully chosen courses. These were International Modernism since 1920, and English Neo-Palladianism. Thus, in the third quarter of the twentieth century Lord Burlington came to have as much influence with young architects as he had 200 years earlier.

In these circumstances, that part of Chiswick House designed by Lord Burlington acquired high intellectual value. Although the whole house was in poor condition and dry rot was evident throughout, it was decided in 1956 to treat John White's wings of 1788 differently from Lord Burlington's nucleus. The wings were demolished and Lord Burlington's architecture was restored by the highest standards of the day. Although the Link Building of *c* 1732 had been refaced when it was absorbed into White's east wing, its interior survived. It was therefore decided to rebuild its exterior from the surviving drawings of Lord Burlington, but in a different stone to make it clear that it formed a secondary phase of the house's development.

The restoration of 1956–57 thus created a house which had never been. Before

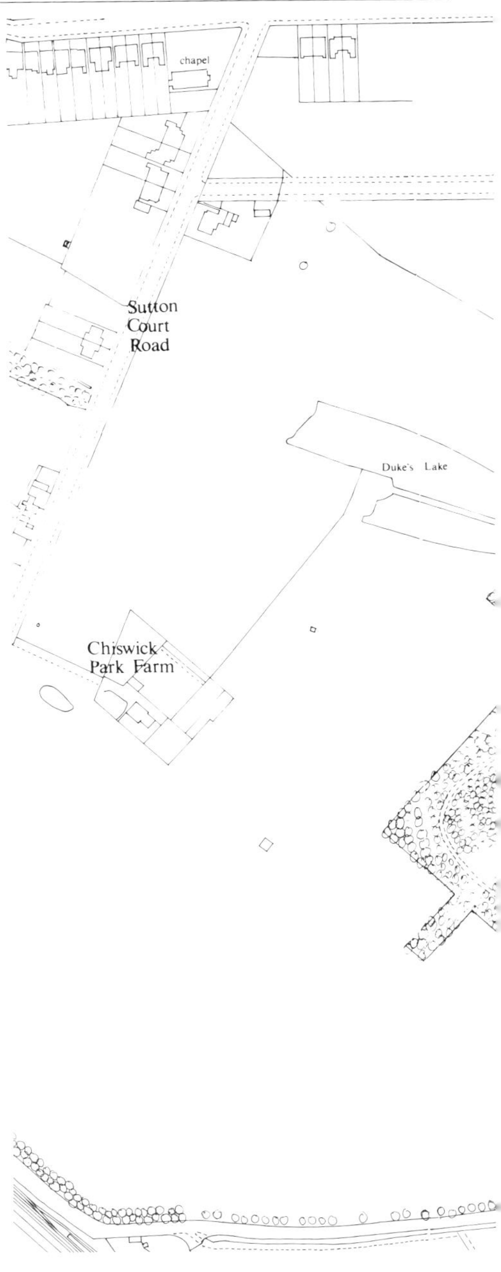

The gardens of Chiswick House in 1895

Avenue
nere Road
gates
lodge
Hogarth Lane
orchard
wall
orchard
Paxton Road
Conservatory
lodge
Chiswick House
vista
River
Burlington Lane
new drive
pool
vista
wall
lodge
N

c 1732 it had not had the Link Building. From *c* 1732 to 1788 it was linked to the old house. From 1788 to 1956 it had become an entirely self-sufficient country house by the addition of the wings. Since 1956, bereft of a kitchen and other office appendages, it has been hard to imagine how the house actually worked.

By the standards of 1956 that was perfectly acceptable, for the house enjoyed its high intellectual status only as the expression of abstract geometrical ideas. Among the historic buildings in the care of the Ministry of Works, however, appraisal based on such criteria was rather an exception, for the Ministry's Inspectorate of Ancient Monuments had always been at pains to appraise monuments in terms of social, as well as intellectual history. Such criteria became still more influential in the 1970s. Simultaneously interest grew in what is called vernacular architecture, small houses which have neither intellectual explanations nor decorative ornament, and which can therefore only be explained in terms of their functional performance. That method of explanation was borrowed from the students of vernacular architecture and applied to the houses of the governing classes by Mark Girouard in a book of 1978 called *Life in the English Country House*. Dr Girouard's book inspired a new policy of interpreting and displaying historic houses as functional organisms rather than as works of art. It is a policy which can never be fully applied to Chiswick House because of the restoration of 1956–57.

Instead, the restoration ensures that Chiswick House will always be a monument to a moment at which art was perceived as purely abstract, and unburdened with the need to perform a service. It demonstrates that remarkable ideology as clearly as Lord Burlington's architecture demonstrates the cultural ambitions of his own time.

GLOSSARY

Apse Semi-circular end of room or church

Arcadian Of pastoral idealism or rustic simplicity

Atrio Vestibule; Italian for the Latin *atrium*, an inner court of a house

Baroque Seventeenth-century art, characterised by clearly unified composition, emphatically expressive of its function.

Capital Uppermost part of column, beneath the entablature

Cascade Series of small waterfalls constructed in a rock garden

Casina A small house or temple in a garden

Coffer Ornamental sunken panel in a ceiling

Colonnade Row of columns supporting an entablature

Commode Low-footed chest in a drawing room

Composite Order One of the Orders (q.v.) invented by the ancient Roman by combining elements from the Ionic and Corinthian Orders

Corinthian Order One of the Orders (q.v.) invented by the ancient Greeks and characterised by bell-shaped capitals ornamented with leaves

Cornice Projecting topmost part of entablature, crowning column, wall, window or door

Cyma Reversa Moulding composed of a double curve (the upper, convex; the lower, concave)

Dentilled Decorated with a series of small rectangular blocks like a row of teeth

Dog Firedog, a metal post used to hold burning wood on a hearth

Doric Greek (and Roman) mode of architectural order, distinguished by its simplicity of design

Elbow Chair Chair with side arms

Entablature Principal horizontal element of an Order, sub-divided into architrave, frieze and cornice

Exedra Large semi-circular recess. Originally, in ancient times, a portico in which disputations were held

Festoon Carved or painted garland of fruit or flowers suspended in a curve between two points

Finial Terminal ornament

Fretwork Geometrical ornament of vertical and horizontal straight lines which overlap to form a continuous patterned band

Frieze Decorative band, or part of entablature between architrave and cornice

Grotesque Decorative style in the manner of ancient Roman grottoes; a work-of-art in which animate forms are fantastically interwoven with decorative foliage

Ha-Ha Sunken wall, set in trench, which excludes animals from a garden, but is invisible to the occupants of a house

Ionic One of the Orders (q.v.) invented by the ancient Greeks and characterised by capitals decorated with spiral scrolls

Knot Garden Flower-bed laid out in an intricate design

Loggia Covered colonnade or arcade which is open to the air on one or more sides

Lutestring Glazed silk fabric

Mannerism Mid sixteenth-century art, characterised by predigious display of classical erudition and exaggerated development of classical forms

Neoclassicism Late eighteenth-century art, characterised by its careful resemblance to the art of classical antiquity

Newel Stair Circular stair with tapering steps winding around a central pillar called a newel

Obelisk Tall, four-sided tapering shaft with, usually, a pyramidal cap

Order System of ornamenting the structural components of classical architecture. There are five Orders: Tuscan, Doric, Ionic, Corinthian and Composite.

Parterre An arrangement of flower-beds

Patte d'oie Three radiating avenues in the shape of a goose's foot

Pergola Framed walk covered by plants

Pier Solid masonry support

Pier Glass Mirror hung between two openings

Porphyry Hard igneous rock with small white and black crystals in red matrix

Portico Covered colonnade forming the entrance to a building

Presence Chamber Room where there is ceremonial attendance upon a king or person of rank

Rococo Early eighteenth-century art, characterised by fragmented composition, artifice and whimsy

Rosery Rose garden

Rusticated Masonry in which courses are emphasised by deeply recessed joints and often have a roughened surface

Serliana Tripartite window, the central opening of which is arched and wider than the side openings which have flat heads. Also called a Venetian or Palladian window

Skyed [Of pictures] Hung high up on a wall

Soffit Underside of a horizontal feature

Sphinx Mythical creature with the head of a woman and the body of a winged lion

Staccato In an abrupt, sharply detached manner

Studiolo Small room in Italian house used for study, or the display of precious objects

Termini Piers or pedestals terminating in a sculptured human bust or face.

Tuscan Order One of the Orders (q.v.), fictively invented by the ancient Etruscans and, in practice, a simplified form of Greek Doric

Venetian Window See Serliana

Vermiculated Rustication Rusticated masonry giving a worm-eaten finish

Vernacular Architecture Native style of building associated with the use of local materials

Vitruvian Scroll Repeating ornamental pattern, like wave crests, used as a frieze.

BIBLIOGRAPHY

Stanley Boorman, 'Lord Burlington and Music', in *Apollo of the Arts : Lord Burlington and his Circle*, Nottingham University Art Gallery, 1973, 16.

Jacques Carré, 'Through French Eyes: Rigaud's Drawings of Chiswick', *Journal of Garden History*, Vol 2, No 2, 133.

Howard Colvin, *Biographical Dictionary of British Architects 1600–1840*, 1978, 61, 75–7, 128–32, 173, 182–5, 309–13, 489–94, 735, 867, 882–3, 940–52.

Howard Colvin, 'Lord Burlington and the Office of Works', in *Lord Burlington and His Circle*, Georgian Group Symposium, 1982, 96.

Timothy Connor, 'Burlingtonian Publications', in *Lord Burlington and His Circle*, Georgian Group Symposium, 1982, 52.

Edward Croft-Murray, *Decorative Painting in England*, Vol 2, 1970, 13–17, 25–9, 200–1, 229–35, 253–6, 264–7.

Daniel Defoe, *A Tour through the Whole Island of Britain*, 2nd edit, 1738, Vol 2, 201.

R and J Dodsley, *Environs of London*, 1761.

Thomas Faulkner, *The History and Antiquities of Brentford, Ealing and Chiswick*, 1845.

John Fleming, *Robert Adam and His Circle*, 1962, 26.

John Harris, *The Artist and the Country House*, 1979, 119, 182–5, 261.

Travers Morgan Planning, unpublished report for the Department of the Environment, *Chiswick House Grounds Historical Survey : Vol 1 (Development of the Grounds)*, 1983.

Fiske Kimball, 'Burlington Architectus', *RIBA Journal*, XXXV, 15 Oct, and 12 Nov 1927.

Pamela Kingsbury, 'Lord Burlington's Architectural Theory and Practice', in *Lord Burlington and His Circle*, Georgian Group Symposium, 1982, 2.

George Knox, 'Sebastiano Ricci at Burlington House: a Venetian decoration "alla Romana"', *Burlington Magazine*, CXXVII, September 1985, 600.

James Lees-Milne, *Earls of Creation*, 1962.

John Macky, *A Journey through England*, 1732, Vol 1, 86.

Treve Rosoman, 'The interior decoration and use of the state apartments of Chiswick House, 1727–70', *Burlington Magazine*, October 1985, 663.

Cinzia Sicca, 'Burlington and Garden Design', in *Lord Burlington and His Circle*, Georgian Group Symposium, 1982, 72.

Cinzia Sicca, 'Lord Burlington at Chiswick: Architecture and Landscape', *Garden History*, Vol 10, No 1, Spring 1982, 36.

Cinzia Sicca, 'On William Kent's Roman Sources', *Architectural History* 29, 1986, 134.

Survey of London, Vol 32, 1963, 390–429, 442–572.

Horace Walpole, Journals of Visits to Country Seats, *Walpole Society*, Vol 16, 1927–8, 22.

M Whiffen, 'New Light on Chiswick', *Architectural Review*, CXIII, April 1953, 269.

Peter Willis, 'Lord Burlington and Landscape Design', in *Apollo of the Arts : Lord Burlington and His Circle*, Nottingham University Art Gallery, 1973, 13.

Rudolf Wittkower, *Palladio and English Neo-Palladianism*, 1974, 114–74.